Scott Foresman Reading

Grade 2

Benchmark Tests Teacher's Manual

Scott Foresman

Editorial Offices: Glenview, Illinois • New York, New York
Sales Offices: Reading, Massachusetts • Duluth, Georgia • Glenview, Illinois
Carrollton, Texas • Menlo Park, California

Editorial Offices
Glenview, Illinois • New York, New York

Sales Offices
Reading, Massachusetts • Duluth, Georgia • Glenview, Illinois
Carrollton, Texas • Menlo Park, California

ISBN 0-673-62405-6

2 3 4 5 6 7 8 9 10-CRK-06 05 04 03 02 01 00

CONTENTS

OVERVIEW

Scott Foresman Reading provides a wide array of formal tests and classroom assessments to support instruction. Formal assessments include the following:

- Placement Tests
- Selection Tests
- Unit Skills Tests and End-of-Year Test
- Unit Benchmark Tests and End-of-Year Test

This Teacher's Manual provides information for administering the Benchmark Tests, scoring the tests, and interpreting the results. Detailed information about other assessment materials and procedures may be found in the *Assessment Handbook.*

Description of the Benchmark Tests

In Grade 2, there are six Unit Benchmark Tests—one for each unit—and an End-of-Year Test. The Unit Benchmark Tests are designed to measure student progress based on the comprehension skills and strategies, literary genres, theme, types of writing, and phonics skills taught in each unit. The End-of-Year Benchmark Test measures skills covered in all six units.

The Benchmark Tests offer an integrated approach to assessment by measuring all skills and strategies in relation to literature selections. These tests provide the kinds of challenging questions and formats found on nationwide standardized tests.

Each Unit Benchmark Test has these features:

- The test has two parts—Part 1: Reading and Part 2: Responding to Literature.
- Part 1 presents two literature selections in different genres. These genres, drawn from fiction, nonfiction, and drama, reflect the focus genres taught in each unit.
- Each literature selection reflects the theme of the unit.
- For each literature selection, there are two Prereading questions in this Teacher's Manual. These questions are designed to activate students' prior knowledge and prepare them to read the selections. Questions begin on page T11.
- Each test has 20 Reading items in both multiple-choice and short-answer formats. These items test reading comprehension, critical thinking skills, literary skills and genre, vocabulary strategies, and phonics skills. Some of the items measure the ability to synthesize information and to compare and contrast across texts.
- Part 2 of each test presents a writing prompt that requires students to respond to one or both of the literature selections. The prompt is based on one of the types of writing taught in the unit.

The End-of-Year Benchmark Test follows the same design as the Unit Benchmark Test, but it offers longer, previously published literature selections and has more items. It measures selected skills from all six units taught during the year.

The Benchmark Tests are designed to assess student progress at the end of each unit and at the end of the school year. Literature selections and questions in the Unit Benchmark Tests become progressively more difficult from Unit 1 to Unit 6, to reflect the increasing sophistication of materials students are expected to handle.

The design of the Benchmark Tests is the result of a two-year development effort, which included the administration of selected tests in a field tryout in the spring of 1998. Results from that field tryout, which involved a representative sample of students across the United States, were used to help refine the tests and ensure an appropriate level of difficulty.

ADMINISTERING THE TESTS

The Benchmark Tests are designed for group administration. You may decide to administer each test in one sitting, or you may administer parts of the test in two or more sittings. (If you administer the test in two or more sittings, try to schedule the sittings on the same day or within a day because some of the questions at the end of the test are based on both literature selections.)

These tests are not intended to be timed. We recommend allowing ample time for all students to complete the tests at their own rates. However, for the purposes of scheduling and planning, the chart below shows the number of items in each test and the estimated amount of time required to complete each section. The Prereading questions are optional and are not scored, but they can be helpful in orienting students to the selections' content and vocabulary. You may choose to read them aloud to your students before they begin reading each selection. (If you include the Prereading questions, allow 5 to 10 additional minutes for each literature selection in Part 1.)

Test Part	Number of Items	Estimated Time
Part 1: Reading Selection 1	10	20–25 minutes
Part 1: Reading Selection 2	10	20–25 minutes
Part 2: Responding to Literature	1 writing prompt	30 minutes

The End-of-Year Benchmark Test has two longer literature selections, a total of 35 items, and one writing prompt. To administer the End-of-Year Benchmark Test, plan on about 75–90 minutes for Part 1 and 30 minutes for Part 2.

Directions for Administering the Tests

In this part of the Teacher's Manual, you will find Prereading questions and directions for administering each Unit Benchmark Test and the End-of-Year Benchmark Test.

Before you administer a test . . .

Review the test to familiarize yourself with the directions and the types of questions. Distribute a test to each student and make sure students have pencils for marking and writing their responses. In Part 1: Reading, students should mark their answers directly on the test pages. In Part 2: Responding to Literature, students will be writing extended responses. They should write their responses on the lines provided. Usually the space should be more than adequate. If students need additional space, however, provide extra lined paper for this purpose.

When you are ready to administer a test . . .

Have students write their names on the test (and on any additional pieces of paper they may use).

- If you choose to administer the Prereading questions, follow the specific directions for each test beginning on page T11.
- If you choose to administer a test without the Prereading questions, use the "General Directions" below.

Directions in **bold** type are intended to be read aloud. Other directions are intended for your information only.

> General Directions
>
> **This is a test about reading and writing. In the first part, you will read two selections and answer some questions about them. There are two kinds of questions in this part. Answer each question by filling in the circle beside the best answer or by writing your answer on the lines. In the second part of the test, you will respond to a writing prompt by writing a short composition.**
>
> Tell students which part(s) of the test they will be expected to complete in each sitting and how much time they have to complete their work. Then direct students to open their booklets to the specified page, read the selection, and answer the questions that follow.

After testing . . .

Directions for scoring the tests begin on page T4. Answer keys begin on page T18.

SCORING THE TESTS

The Benchmark Tests are intended to be scored by part—a total score for Part 1: Reading and a separate score for Part 2: Responding to Literature. To make scoring easier, copy and use the following charts as needed:

- the Unit Benchmark Test Evaluation Chart on page T8, for recording an individual student's scores on a Unit Benchmark Test;
- the End-of-Year Benchmark Test Evaluation Chart on page T9, for recording an individual student's scores on an End-of-Year Benchmark Test;
- the Class Record Chart on page T10, for recording test scores for all students for all six units.

Answer Keys for each test begin on page T18. In Part 1, there are two types of items: multiple choice and short answer. These types of questions are scored in slightly different ways, as explained below. For the writing prompt in Part 2, the Answer Key provides a scoring guide based on a scale of 1 to 4.

Scoring Multiple-Choice Items

Each multiple-choice item has four answer choices labeled A, B, C, D. Referring to the Answer Key for the test, mark each multiple-choice item correct or incorrect.

Scoring Short-Answer Items

Score the response to each short-answer item as correct or incorrect. There is no partial credit given for partly correct responses. However, to evaluate responses to the short-answer items, you will need to be familiar with the literature selections in the test. By nature, short-answer items are somewhat open-ended and may be interpreted in different ways. The suggested answers provided for the short-answer items are generally examples of correct responses; they are not intended to be the only acceptable answers. To evaluate some responses, you will need to use your judgment. If the student's response does not match the suggested answer but seems to be a reasonable response, give the student the benefit of the doubt and mark the response correct.

Example
The Unit 1 Benchmark Test includes this question about the first selection, "The Wedding Band":
Question: How was Dog a special friend to Pig? Tell something Dog did that shows he was a good friend.

The Answer Key says, "Wording may vary. Possible answers: Dog helped Pig by getting a band for his wedding, or by doing whatever Pig needed."

If a student answers "He got a band," this is a correct response. It does not use the same wording as the Answer Key, but it clearly reflects an understanding of the selection and what Dog did.

A response that says "He went to the wedding" or "He got a ring" should be marked incorrect. These responses do not tell what Dog did that showed he was a special friend and do not reflect an understanding of the selection.

Scoring Part 2: Responding to Literature

The second part of the test requires an extended written response, such as a personal narrative or a how-to report, based on one or both of the literature selections. To evaluate the students' responses, you will need to be familiar with both the writing prompt and the literature selections. To score a response, review the Scoring Guide provided in the Answer Key. Then read the student's writing and score it on a scale of 1 to 4, based on the criteria described in the Scoring Guide.

The criteria provided in each Scoring Guide are based on the content of one or both literature selections and the key features of specific kinds of writing—as they have been taught in the Writing Process activities. The 4-point scale reflects the general levels of performance defined below; these levels are defined more specifically for each Responding to Literature activity.

Scoring Guides: 4-Point Scale

4 Exemplary

An "exemplary" piece of writing reflects a clear understanding of the literature selection(s) and includes all the key features required for the specific type of writing. Errors in grammar, usage, and mechanics are minimal and do not affect meaning.

3 Competent

A "competent" piece of writing reflects an understanding of the literature selection(s) and includes most of the key features required for the specific type of writing. It may include a few errors in grammar, usage, and mechanics, but they do not affect meaning.

2 Developing

A "developing" piece of writing reflects some understanding of the literature selection(s) and includes some key features required for the specific type of writing. It may include several errors in grammar, usage, and mechanics, which may affect meaning.

1 Emerging

An "emerging" piece of writing needs improvement. It reflects little understanding of the literature selection(s) and does not include key features required for the specific type of writing. Errors in grammar, usage, and mechanics obscure meaning.

Using an Evaluation Chart

On pages T8 and T9 you will find two Evaluation Charts. The Unit Benchmark Test Evaluation Chart may be used to score any of the Unit Benchmark Tests; the End-of-Year chart may be used to score the End-of-Year Benchmark Test.

To score a Benchmark Test using an Evaluation Chart, we recommend the following procedure:

1. Make a copy of the appropriate Evaluation Chart for each student.
2. Refer to the Answer Key for the test you are scoring.
3. In Part 1, mark the response to each question correct or incorrect. (There is no partial credit given for partly correct responses.) On the Evaluation Chart, circle the question number for each item answered correctly and draw an X through the number of each question answered incorrectly.
4. To find the total score for Part 1, add the number of items answered correctly.
5. To determine a percentage score for the number of items answered correctly, use one of the tables below (for the Unit Benchmark Tests or the End-of-Year Benchmark Test).
6. For Part 2, review the Scoring Guide provided in the Answer Key. Then read the student's writing and score it on a scale of 1 to 4, based on the criteria described in the Scoring Guide.
7. Mark the student's score for writing on the Evaluation Chart. Add any notes or observations about the writing that may be helpful to you and the student in later instruction.

Table 1. Percentage Scores for Unit Benchmark Tests			
Number Correct	**Percentage Score**	**Number Correct**	**Percentage Score**
1	5%	11	55%
2	10%	12	60%
3	15%	13	65%
4	20%	14	70%
5	25%	15	75%
6	30%	16	80%
7	35%	17	85%
8	40%	18	90%
9	45%	19	95%
10	50%	20	100%

Table 2. Percentage Scores for End-of-Year Benchmark Tests					
Number Correct	Percentage Score	Number Correct	Percentage Score	Number Correct	Percentage Score
1	3%	13	37%	25	71%
2	6%	14	40%	26	74%
3	9%	15	43%	27	77%
4	11%	16	46%	28	80%
5	14%	17	49%	29	83%
6	17%	18	51%	30	86%
7	20%	19	54%	31	89%
8	23%	20	57%	32	91%
9	26%	21	60%	33	94%
10	29%	22	63%	34	97%
11	31%	23	66%	35	100%
12	34%	24	69%		

Interpreting Test Results

A student's score on the Benchmark Test provides only one look at a student's progress and should be interpreted in conjunction with other assessments and the teacher's observations. However, a low score on one or both parts of the Benchmark Test probably indicates a need for closer review of the student's performance and perhaps additional instruction.

For these Benchmark Tests, we recommend a passing score of at least 70% on Part 1 and, for Part 2, a score of at least 2 on the 4-point scale. For students who do not achieve these scores on the two parts of the test, you may want to review the students' responses more carefully. On pages T26–29, you will find a list of tested skills for each Benchmark Test. By identifying which items the student answered incorrectly and referring to the list of tested skills, you may be able to determine skills or specific areas in which the student needs additional help. For example, if the student answers six questions incorrectly and all six involve literary elements such as plot and character, then you may want to plan additional instruction for the student in this area.

Grading. If you would like more information on how to use a writing assessment scale for determining grades, refer to the "Grading Writing" section of the *Assessment Handbook*.

EVALUATION CHART

Unit Benchmark Test

Student Name ____ **Unit** ________________

Part/Item Numbers				Number Correct	Percentage Score
Part 1: Reading					
1	6	11	16		
2	7	12	17		
3	8	13	18		
4	9	14	19		
5	10	15	20		

Part 2: Responding to Literature	Score
Type of Writing:	1 2 3 4

Notes/Observations

Evaluation Chart

End-of-Year Benchmark Test

Student Name ____ **Date** _______________

Part/Item Numbers					Number Correct	Percentage Score
Part 1: Reading						
1	8	15	22	29		
2	9	16	23	30		
3	10	17	24	31		
4	11	18	25	32		
5	12	19	26	33		
6	13	20	27	34		
7	14	21	28	35		

Part 2: Responding to Literature	Score
Type of Writing:	1 2 3 4

Notes/Observations

CLASS RECORD CHART

Unit Benchmark Tests

Teacher Name _______________________________ **Class** _________________

Student Name	Unit 1		Unit 2		Unit 3		Unit 4		Unit 5		Unit 6	
	Pt1	Pt2	Pt1	Pt2	Pt1	Pt2	Pt1	Pt2	Pt1	Pt2	Pt1	Pt2

You + Me = Special

This is a test about reading and writing. In the first part, you will read two stories and answer some questions about them.

Part 1: Reading

Prereading Questions: "The Wedding Band"

Let's begin with the first story. Open your tests to page 1 and listen to these questions.

A.   Look at the picture on the first page. Do you think this story is about something real or make-believe? Tell why you think so.

Encourage students to tell whether they think the story is about something real or make-believe and why they think so. For example, students might say it is about something make-believe because the pig is wearing clothes or the dog is riding a bike.

B.   The story is called "The Wedding Band." What happens at a wedding?

Have students explain that people get married at a wedding. They might also mention other things that people do at weddings, such as eating cake or dancing.

Questions 1–7
Have students read "The Wedding Band" and answer questions 1–7. When they have finished, have them read the directions for questions 8–10 on page 6.

Questions 8–10
The next three questions are about letters and sounds. I am going to say a word and ask you to find the word that has the same sounds. Listen carefully.

8.   Look at the three words. In the story, Dog's band began to <u>play</u>. Which word has the same beginning sounds as <u>play</u> . . . <u>play</u>?

9.   When Miss Patsy arrived, <u>she</u> said hooray! Which word has the same beginning sound as <u>she</u> . . . <u>she</u>?

10.   Now I'm going to ask you to listen to the ending sound. Look at the three words. Miss Patsy had a <u>ring</u>. Which word has the same ending sound as <u>ring</u> . . . <u>ring</u>?

Prereading Questions: "Jumping Jessica"

Let's go on to the second story. Turn to page 7 in your tests and listen to these questions.

C.   Look at the picture and think about the title. What do you think this story is about?

Have students suggest what they think the story is about. For example, it is about a girl who likes to jump rope.

D.   What do you want to find out when you read this story?

Encourage students to tell what they want to find out, such as what happens to the girl or why she likes to jump rope.

Questions 11–20
Have students read "Jumping Jessica" and answer questions 11–20. When they have finished, proceed with the Responding to Literature activity.

Part 2: Responding to Literature

Have students turn to page 12. Read the writing prompt aloud. Have students write their responses on the lines provided.

Zoom In!

This is a test about reading and writing. In the first part, you will read two stories and answer some questions about them.

Part 1: Reading

Prereading Questions: "Wonders of the Woods"

Let's begin with the first story. Open your tests to page 1 and listen to these questions.

A. **Look at the picture of Ranger Joe. He is standing beside a sign that says "Nature Trail." What do you think this story is about?**

Encourage students to tell what they think the story is about. For example, they might say it is about exploring or walking through the woods.

B. **Think about walking in the woods. What are some things you can see and hear in the woods?**

Have students describe sights and sounds of the woods.

Questions 1–10
Have students read "Wonders of the Woods" and answer questions 1–10. Then continue in the same way with the second selection.

Prereading Questions: "A Special Farm"

Let's go on to the second story. Turn to page 6 in your tests and listen to these questions.

C. **This story is called "A Special Farm." The farm is in a town called Barra del Colorado in a small country called Costa Rica, which is far from here. What would you like to find out about this farm when you read the story?**

Have students suggest things they would like to find out about this farm. For example, they may want to find out why it is special or what is grown on the farm.

D. **What do you know about butterflies? Tell me one or two things you know about butterflies.**

Encourage students to tell what they know about butterflies.

Questions 11–20
Have students read "A Special Farm" and answer questions 11–20. When they have finished, proceed with the Responding to Literature activity.

Part 2: Responding to Literature

Have students turn to page 12. Read the writing prompt aloud. Have students write their responses on the lines provided.

Side by Side

This is a test about reading and writing. In the first part, you will read two stories and answer some questions about them.

Part 1: Reading

Prereading Questions: "The Line"

Let's begin with the first story. Open your tests to page 1 and listen to these questions.

A. Look at the picture and read the title of the story. What do you think this story is going to be about?

Encourage students to tell what they think the story is about. For example, they might say it is about two sisters who do not get along.

B. What do you want to find out when you read this story?

Have students tell what they want to find out, such as what "the line" is.

Questions 1–10
Have students read "The Line" and answer questions 1–10. Then continue in the same way with the second selection.

Prereading Questions: "Who Cut Them Down?"

Let's go on to the second story. Turn to page 7 in your tests and listen to these questions.

C. Look at the picture and think about the title. What do you think will happen in this story?

Have students predict what will happen in this story. For example, students might say that the trees will be cut down.

D. What kind of story do you think this is?

Have students tell what kind of story they think this is. For example, students might think it is a mystery, a fantasy, or a nonfiction piece about squirrels.

Questions 11–20
Have students read "Who Cut Them Down?" and answer questions 11–20. When they have finished, proceed with the Responding to Literature activity.

Part 2: Responding to Literature

Have students turn to page 12. Read the writing prompt aloud. Have students write their responses on the lines provided.

Ties Through Time

This is a test about reading and writing. In the first part, you will read two stories and answer some questions about them.

Part 1: Reading

Prereading Questions: "Marching On"

Let's begin with the first story. Open your tests to page 1 and listen to these questions.

A.   Look at the picture and read the title of the story. What do you think this story is about?

Have students tell what they think the story is about. For example, it is about a parade or about Founder's Day.

B.   What are some reasons for having a parade?

Have students discuss reasons for having a parade, such as celebrating a holiday or honoring someone.

Questions 1–10
Have students read "Marching On" and answer questions 1–10. Then continue in the same way with the second selection.

Prereading Questions:
"Deer Hunter and White Corn Maiden"

Let's go on to the second story. Turn to page 6 in your tests and listen to these questions.

C.   This story is called "Deer Hunter and White Corn Maiden." From this title, what can you tell about the two main characters in this story?

Encourage students to discuss what they can tell from the title. For example, the main characters are Native Americans, or the story is about a hunter and a maiden.

D.   This story tells about traditions. A tradition is something we do together in a special way. Traditions are often handed down from grandparents and parents to children. Who can think of an example of a tradition?

Have students give examples of traditions, or give some examples to make sure children understand what traditions are. Examples: having turkey on Thanksgiving, putting candles on birthday cakes, wearing nice clothes for special occasions.

Questions 11–20
Have students read "Deer Hunter and White Corn Maiden" and answer questions 11–20. When they have finished, proceed with the Responding to Literature activity.

Part 2: Responding to Literature

Have students turn to page 12. Read the writing prompt aloud. Have students write their responses on the lines provided.

All Aboard!

This is a test about reading and writing. In the first part, you will read two selections and answer some questions about them.

Part 1: Reading

Prereading Questions: "Friends Far from Home"

Let's begin with the first story. Open your tests to page 1 and listen to these questions.

A.   Look at the picture and read the title. What do you think this story is about?

Have students tell what they think the story is about. For example, it is about a girl and her mother who have car trouble.

B.   What do you think will happen in this story?

Have students predict what they think will happen. For example, the girl and her mother will go to find help, or they will meet new friends.

Questions 1–10
Have students read "Friends Far from Home" and answer questions 1–10. Then continue in the same way with the second selection.

Prereading Questions: "Traveling Back in Time"

Let's go on to the second selection. Turn to page 6 in your tests and listen to these questions.

C.   Look at the picture. This selection is called "Traveling Back in Time." What do you think this selection is about?

Encourage students to tell what they think the selection is about. For example, they might think it is about taking a long trip or about what life was like long ago.

D.   What do you know about living on a farm? Tell me one or two jobs you know that children could do on a farm.

Have students tell some things they know about living on a farm—in particular, some jobs that children could do.

Questions 11–20
Have students read "Traveling Back in Time" and answer questions 11–20. When they have finished, proceed with the Responding to Literature activity.

Part 2: Responding to Literature

Have students turn to page 12. Read the writing prompt aloud. Have students write their responses on the lines provided.

Just Imagine!

This is a test about reading and writing. In the first part, you will read two selections and answer some questions about them.

Part 1: Reading

Prereading Questions: "A Clean Sweep"

Let's begin with the first story. Open your tests to page 1 and listen to these questions.

A.   Take a quick look at the selection. What kind of selection do you think this is?

Have students point out that this is a play. If they do not realize that it is a play, tell them.

B.   What do you think will happen in this play?

Have students predict what they think will happen. For example, the messy room will be cleaned up.

Questions 1–10
Have students read "A Clean Sweep" and answer questions 1–10. Then continue in the same way with the second selection.

Prereading Questions: "The Oddball Race"

Let's go on to the second story. Turn to page 7 in your tests and listen to these questions.

C.   This story is called "The Oddball Race." From this title, what can you tell about the story?

Encourage students to discuss what they can tell from the title. For example, the story is about some kind of race.

D.   What do you want to find out when you read this story?

Have students set purposes for reading by telling what they want to find out, such as what kind of race it is or who wins the race.

Questions 11–20
Have students read "The Oddball Race" and answer questions 11–20. When they have finished, proceed with the Responding to Literature activity.

Part 2: Responding to Literature

Have students turn to page 12. Read the writing prompt aloud. Have students write their responses on the lines provided.

PREREADING QUESTIONS AND DIRECTIONS, END-OF-YEAR TEST

This is a test about reading and writing. In the first part, you will read two selections and answer some questions about them.

Part 1: Reading

Prereading Questions: "Linda's Invention"

Let's begin with the first story. Open your tests to page 1 and listen to these questions.

A.   The title of this story is "Linda's Invention." What is an invention?

Have students tell what an invention is. For example, it is an original idea or a new thing made for a specific purpose.

B.   What do you think will happen in this story?

Have students predict what they think will happen. For example, a person named Linda will invent something.

Questions 1–17
Have students read "Linda's Invention" and answer questions 1–17. Then continue in the same way with the second selection.

Prereading Questions: "About Dr. Seuss"

Let's go on to the second selection. Turn to page 11 in your tests and listen to these questions.

C.   This selection is called "About Dr. Seuss." Can you name any books written by Dr. Seuss?

Encourage students to name books written by Dr. Seuss, such as *The Cat in the Hat* and *How the Grinch Stole Christmas.*

D.   What do you want to find out when you read this selection?

Have students set purposes for reading by telling what they want to find out, such as how Dr. Seuss came up with his ideas or how he wrote his books.

Questions 18–35
Have students read "About Dr. Seuss" and answer questions 18–35. When they have finished, proceed with the Responding to Literature activity.

Part 2: Responding to Literature

Have students turn to page 20. Read the writing prompt aloud. Have students write their responses on the lines provided.

You + Me = Special

Unit 1 Benchmark Test

Name _______________________________

Date _______________________________

Copyright © Addison-Wesley Educational Publishers Inc.

All rights reserved. Printed in the United States of America.

The blackline masters in this book may be duplicated for classroom use only without further permission from the publisher.

This publication is protected by Copyright and permission should be obtained from the publisher prior to any prohibited reproduction, storage in a retrieval system, or transmission in any form or by any means, electronic, mechanical, photocopying, recording, or otherwise. For information regarding permission, write to: Scott Foresman, 1900 East Lake Avenue, Glenview, Illinois 60025.

Editorial Offices
Glenview, Illinois • New York, New York

Sales Offices
Reading, Massachusetts • Duluth, Georgia • Glenview, Illinois
Carrollton, Texas • Menlo Park, California

ISBN 0-673-62368-8

2 3 4 5 6 7 8 9 10-ML-06 05 04 03 02 01 00

The Wedding Band

by M. S. Peterson

Pig came down the road. He had a big smile on his face.

Along came Dog on his bike. "Why are you so happy, Pig?" he asked.

"It's a beautiful day," said Pig. "The sun is shining. The apple trees are in bloom. And Miss Patsy says she will marry me! Our wedding will be tomorrow at noon."

Suddenly Pig did not look happy. "Oh, pickles," he said. "Tomorrow is very soon. How can I be ready in time?"

"Maybe I can help you," said Dog.

"Oh, thank you, Dog!" said Pig. "Yes, yes, you can help. I must get a wedding band. Could you find me a nice wedding band by tomorrow noon?"

Dog said he could, and off he rode.

The next day, Pig heard a loud noise outside his house. He opened the window. His friends were making music.

"Here is the band for your wedding, Pig," said Dog. "I hope you like it."

"Oh, pickles," said Pig. "I didn't mean that kind of wedding band. I need a wedding ring!"

Just then, Miss Patsy came by. "Hooray! Here is a band to play at our wedding!" she said. "Dear Pig, this is a wonderful surprise. Oh, I can hardly wait to dance!"

GO ON ▶

Miss Patsy's mother and father came along behind her. Her grandmother came too.

"Oh, dear," said Miss Patsy, "I forgot to tell you. My grandmother has a gold ring. She wants us to have it for the wedding. I hope you don't mind."

"Pickles!" said Pig. "I don't mind at all."

Pig and Patsy were married outside Pig's house. Then they cut the wedding cake.

Everyone ate cake. Then Dog's wonderful wedding band began to play.

Patsy stood up and took Mr. Pig by the hoof. "Come on, Pig," she said. "Let's dance!"

GO ON ➤

Questions 1–7. Fill in the circle beside the best answer to each question, or write your answer on the lines.

1. What will Miss Patsy and Pig do next?
   (A) They will dance.
   (B) They will cut the cake.
   (C) They will go to a wedding.

2. How did Pig feel when he first met Dog?
   (A) very happy
   (B) afraid
   (C) very sad

3. Where did Pig and Dog meet?

____

____

GO ON

4. What made Pig feel unhappy?
  Ⓐ He could not find Miss Patsy.
  Ⓑ He did not have a ring.
  Ⓒ Dog would not help him.

5. Where did the wedding take place?

____

- -

____

- -

____

6. The author wrote this story to
  Ⓐ give facts about pigs.
  Ⓑ show how to make a wedding cake.
  Ⓒ tell about something funny.

7. How was Dog a special friend to Pig? Tell
something Dog did that shows he was a good
friend.

____

- -

____

- -

____

STOP

8. Ⓐ blue   Ⓑ slow   Ⓒ plan

9. Ⓐ skip   Ⓑ shake   Ⓒ see

10. Ⓐ land   Ⓑ long   Ⓒ look

STOP

Jumping Jessica

by M. S. Peterson

Jessica liked to jump rope. One day she took her jump rope to school. When her class went outside at recess, Jessica started jumping.

"One potato, two potato, three potato, four," she sang. She liked jumping to the sound of the words. But she wished she had a friend jumping with her.

The next day, Jessica took her jump rope to school again. At recess, she saw someone else with a jump rope. Her name was Claire.

"Miss Mary Mack, Mack, Mack," Claire was singing as she jumped. It was a song that Jessica knew.

Jessica started jumping with her. "All dressed in black, black, black," they both sang.

The two girls jumped rope together every day. They did lots of different jumps.

Then one day Jessica got a long rope and tied one end to a post. Jessica and Claire took turns. One jumped and one turned the rope. "This isn't working very well," said Jessica. "We really need three people for this."

They put away the long rope.

The next day, a new girl came to school. Her name was Marie. She had a big cast on her leg. Her leg was broken.

Every day the new girl sat and watched Jessica and Claire. She seemed sad. She never smiled.

A week later, Marie came to school without the cast. Her leg was better.

Jessica had an idea. At recess, she got out the long rope and walked over to Marie. "Would you like to join us?" she asked.

"I would love to," said Marie with a big smile.

Questions 11–20. Fill in the circle beside the best answer to each question, or write your answer on the lines.

11. What will happen next in this story?
    Ⓐ Jessica will get a cast on her leg.
    Ⓑ Marie will jump rope with the other girls.
    Ⓒ The three girls will play baseball.

12. Where does this story take place?
    Ⓐ at a school playground
    Ⓑ at Jessica's house
    Ⓒ at Claire's house

13. Which word best tells about Jessica?
    Ⓐ quiet
    Ⓑ mean
    Ⓒ friendly

GO ON ➤

14. Why was Jessica happy to meet Claire?

    Ⓐ She liked to jump with a friend.

    Ⓑ Claire had a long rope.

    Ⓒ She broke her leg.

15. The author wrote this story to

    Ⓐ show how to jump rope.

    Ⓑ tell what happened to three girls.

    Ⓒ teach the words to songs for jumping rope.

16. This story tells about

    Ⓐ things that could not really happen.

    Ⓑ people who could be real.

    Ⓒ something that happened a long time ago.

17. The story says, "A <u>week</u> later, Marie came to school without the cast." Which word has the same sound as the <u>ee</u> in <u>week</u>?

    Ⓐ tied

    Ⓑ they

    Ⓒ team

18. Jessica liked to jump <u>rope</u>. Which word has the same long <u>o</u> sound as <u>rope</u>?

Ⓐ home

Ⓑ song

Ⓒ school

19. From this story, what do you know about Jessica that makes her special? Name one thing you know about her that makes her special.

____
____
____
____

20. Think about the two stories you have read: "The Wedding Band" and "Jumping Jessica." How are the friends in them alike? Write a sentence telling how they are alike.

____
____
____
____

STOP

PART 2: RESPONDING TO LITERATURE

In each of the two stories you have read, something
special happens. Pig and Miss Patsy get married,
and Jessica finds some new friends. Think about
something special that has happened to you. You
might have met a new friend or learned to do
something new.

Write a story telling about something special that
has happened to you. Make sure your story has a
beginning, middle, and end. It should have three or
four sentences. Write your story for a friend to read.

GO ON ▶

STOP

Zoom In!

Unit 2 Benchmark Test

Name ______________________________

Date ______________________________

Scott Foresman
Reading
Grade 2

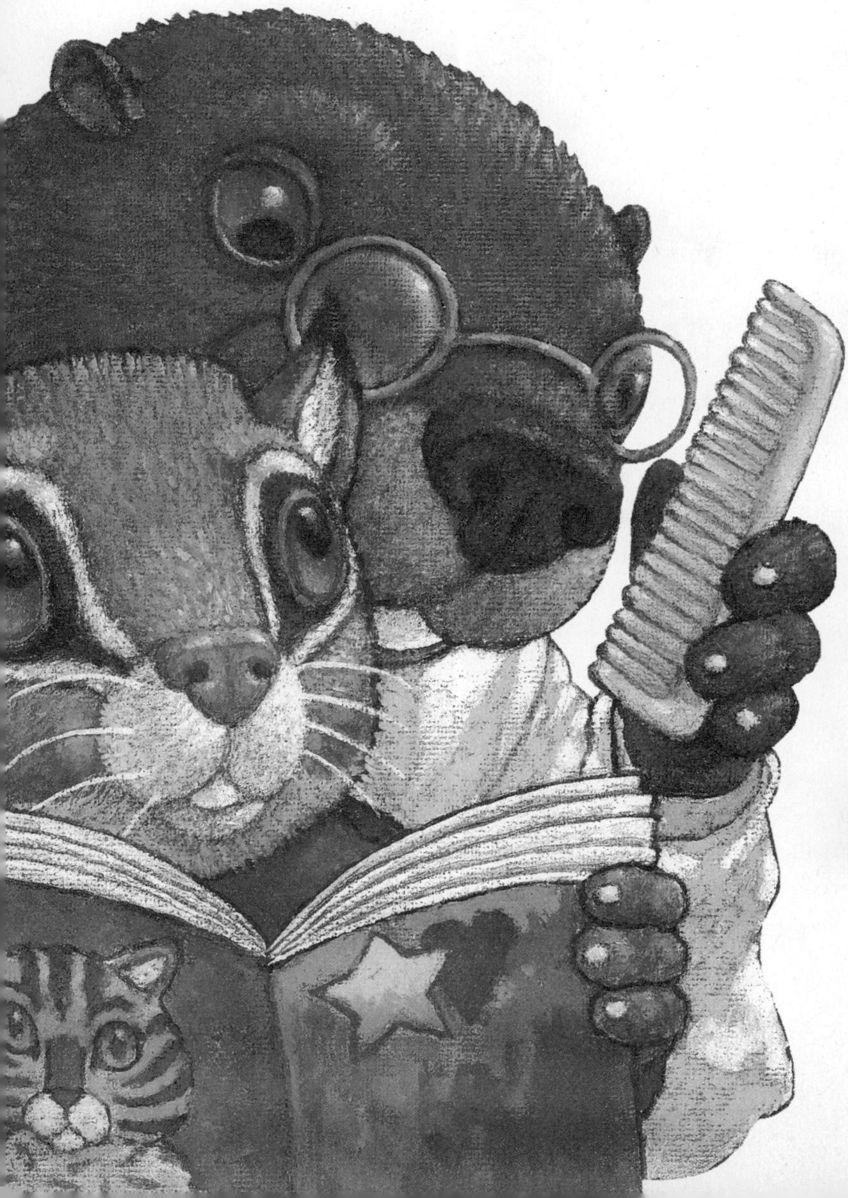

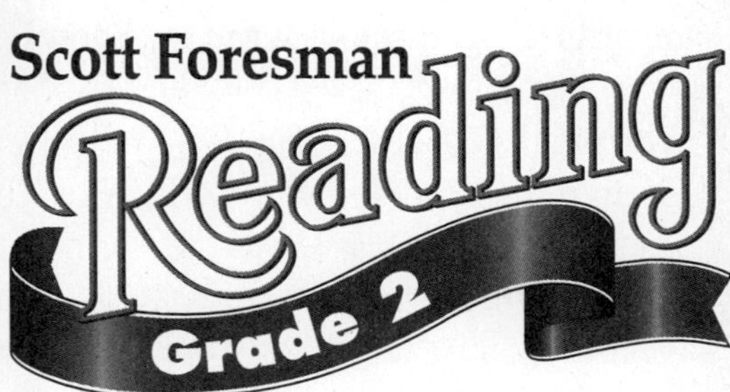

Editorial Offices
Glenview, Illinois • New York, New York

Sales Offices
Reading, Massachusetts • Duluth, Georgia • Glenview, Illinois
Carrollton, Texas • Menlo Park, California

ISBN 0-673-62369-6

2 3 4 5 6 7 8 9 10-ML-06 05 04 03 02 01 00

Wonders of the Woods

by Janet Callahan

Welcome to the Nature Trail. My name is Ranger Joe. I will lead you on a walk through the woods. Let's follow this path.

Do you see the ferns growing along the path? They look alike at first. But look more closely. There are tall ferns and short ones. Some have rounded leaves. Others have pointed leaves.

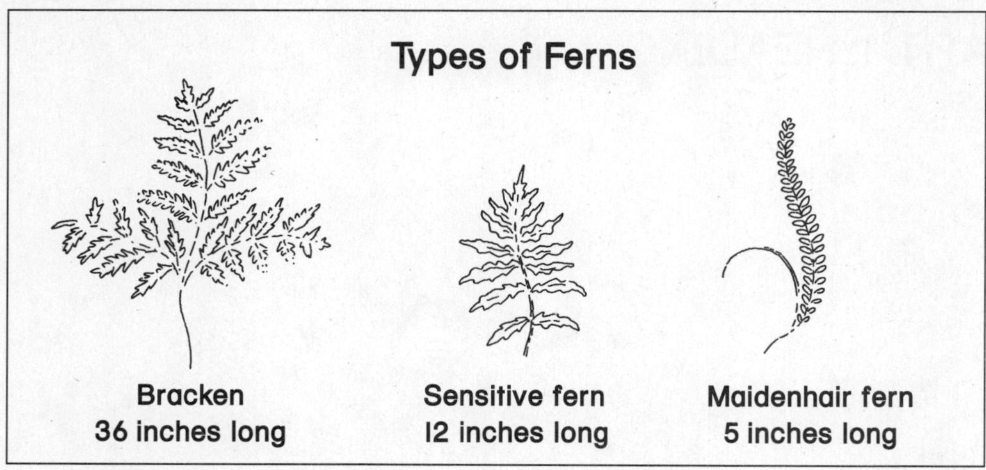

Stop now. What can you hear? You can hear birds singing. You can hear insects chirping. There is another sound too. Is it the wind? No, it can't be. The tree branches are still. Walk this way. The sound is getting loud. What do you think it is?

Climb up this bank and look down. The sound you hear is a brook. You can tell there has been a lot of rain because the water is high, and it is flowing fast. Notice the animal tracks in the mud. One set looks like small hand prints. They were made by a raccoon. The others were made by a deer.

Let's keep going. Do you see the fallen tree on the right? The tree is slowly rotting, but it is also full of life. Look inside and you'll see. This tree is full of bugs, worms, and other small creatures. Some of them eat the wood. Others eat the tiny plants that grow on the wood.

Now we have come to the end of our walk. Please come back soon. There are always new things to see here in the woods.

Questions 1–10. Fill in the circle beside the best answer to each question, or write your answer on the lines.

1. When he begins to walk, what does Ranger Joe point out first on the path?
   - Ⓐ ferns
   - Ⓑ a brook
   - Ⓒ animal tracks

2. Look at the picture on page 2. Which fern is five inches long?

   ____

   -

   ____

   -

   ____

3. What do the feet of a raccoon look like?
   - Ⓐ mittens
   - Ⓑ small hands
   - Ⓒ tree branches

GO ON

4. How does Ranger Joe find the brook?

  Ⓐ He uses a map.

  Ⓑ He reads a sign.

  Ⓒ He follows the sound of water.

5. Suppose it does not rain for weeks. What is one way in which the brook will be different?

____

____

____

6. "Wonders of the Woods" is mostly about

  Ⓐ finding a brook.

  Ⓑ looking for bugs.

  Ⓒ learning about nature.

7. Which word best tells about Ranger Joe?

  Ⓐ helpful

  Ⓑ quiet

  Ⓒ shy

8. Ranger Joe says, "Walk this <u>way</u>." Which word has the same long <u>a</u> sound as <u>way</u>?

(A) pan

(B) pain

(C) pen

9. There is a fa<u>ll</u>en tree on the ground. Which word has the same sound as the underlined letters in fa<u>ll</u>en?

(A) moving

(B) when

(C) below

10. Which word best fits in this sentence?

Ranger Joe _________ in the woods.

(A) walks

(B) walk's

(C) walking

STOP

A Special Farm

by Janet Callahan

When you think of farm animals, you may think of cows or sheep. But in a little town in Costa Rica called Barra del Colorado, the "farm animals" are butterflies. And the farmers are children!

For many years, people in Barra del Colorado made a living by fishing. But each year, there were fewer fish. The people needed a new way to make money.

A woman named Brent Davies had a plan. She knew a lot about butterflies, and she wanted to help the town raise some. Many butterflies live in the rainforest nearby. Brent knew that zoos would pay for the butterflies.

Brent talked to people at the school in the town. They let her use the schoolyard for her farm. The children would be her helpers.

First, Brent and the children planted special flowers and plants that butterflies like. Before long, butterflies came to the flowers. They began laying eggs on the plants. From the eggs came caterpillars.

A Butterfly's Life

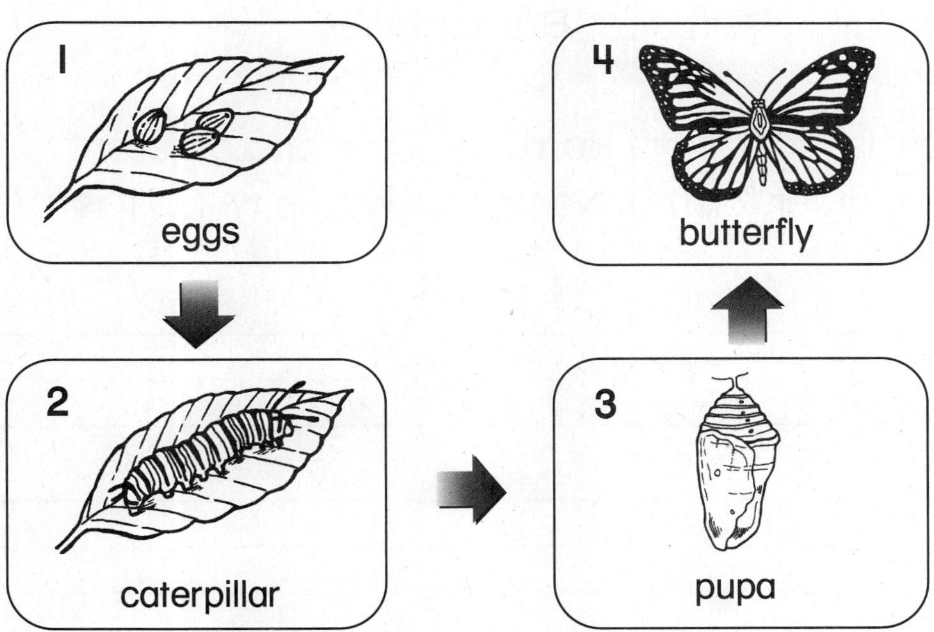

The children collected caterpillars from the plants. They put them in cages filled with leaves. Each caterpillar soon turned into a pupa.

The children mailed the pupae to a zoo. There, the pupae turned into butterflies.

The money the children made helped the whole town.

11. What did the people of Barra del Colorado need to do?

    Ⓐ learn how to raise fish

    Ⓑ find a new way to make money

    Ⓒ build a home for Brent Davies

12. How is the farm in Barra del Colorado different from other farms? Name one way in which it is different.

____

____

____

____

13. When the children started the farm, what did they do first?

    Ⓐ They filled cages with leaves.

    Ⓑ They collected caterpillars.

    Ⓒ They planted flowers and plants that butterflies like.

14. Look at the picture on page 7. What is a butterfly called in the third part of its life?

____

- -

____

15. What did the children do last?
Ⓐ They mailed the pupae to a zoo.
Ⓑ They collected caterpillars.
Ⓒ They filled cages with leaves.

16. For the people of Barra del Colorado, what was the best thing about the butterfly farm?
Ⓐ It kept the children busy.
Ⓑ It gave them a way to make money.
Ⓒ It made school more interesting.

GO ON

17. What is another good title for what you just read?

   Ⓐ "Going to School"

   Ⓑ "At the Zoo"

   Ⓒ "Raising Butterflies"

18. You read about Brent that "The children would be <u>her</u> helpers." Which word has the same sounds as the <u>er</u> in <u>her</u>?

   Ⓐ are

   Ⓑ turn

   Ⓒ for

19. Which is a compound word?

   Ⓐ animals

   Ⓑ fishing

   Ⓒ schoolyard

GO ON

20. Think about the people you have read about:
Ranger Joe in "Wonders of the Woods" and
Brent Davies in "A Special Farm." What is one
way in which Ranger Joe and Brent Davies are
alike?

____

____

____

____

PART 2: RESPONDING TO LITERATURE

In this test, you have read about a nature trail and a butterfly farm. If you could go to one of these places, which one would you choose? What would you see there?

Choose one of the places. Write three or four sentences to describe the place. Tell what you would see if you went there. You might also tell what you would hear and smell.

Write your sentences for a friend to read.

GO ON ▶

Side by Side

Unit 3 Benchmark Test

Name ______________________________

Date ______________________________

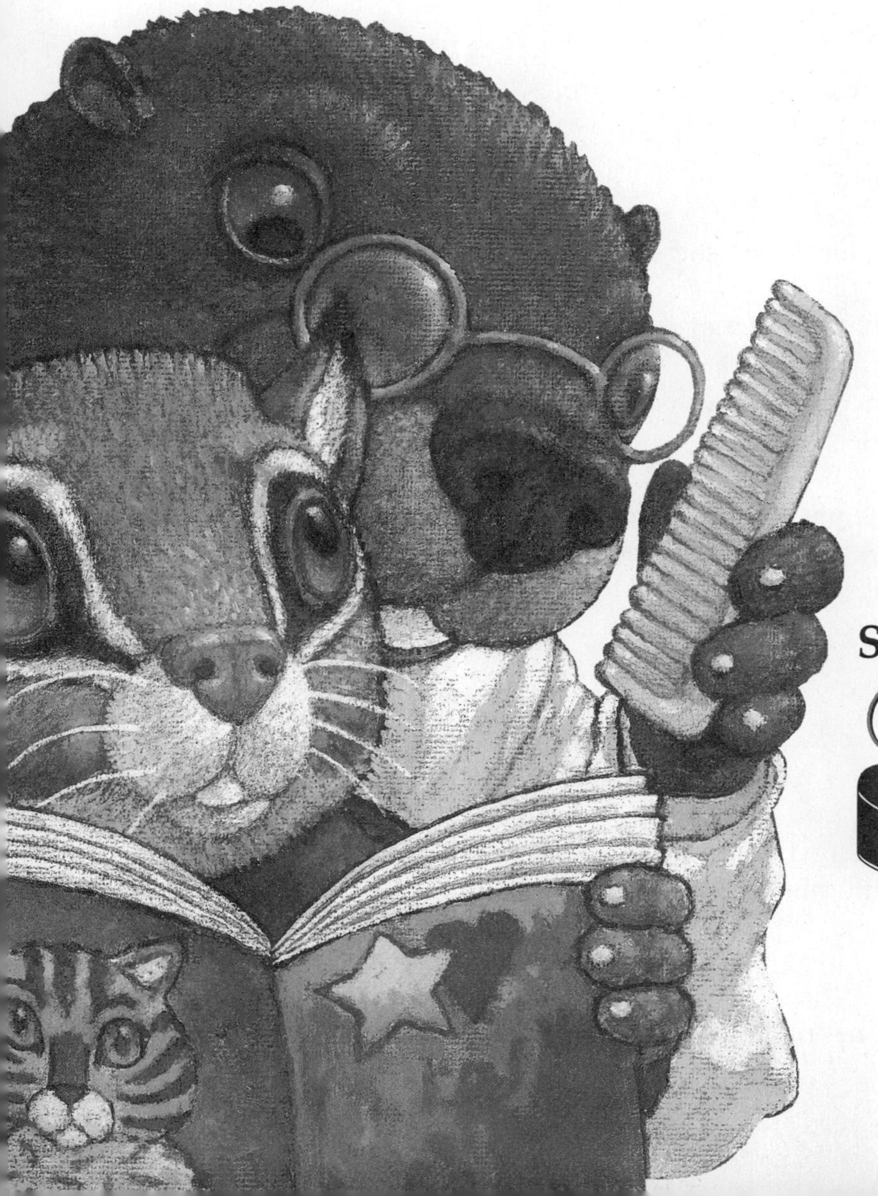

Scott Foresman Reading Grade 2

Editorial Offices
Glenview, Illinois • New York, New York

Sales Offices
Reading, Massachusetts • Duluth, Georgia • Glenview, Illinois
Carrollton, Texas • Menlo Park, California

ISBN 0-673-62370-X

2 3 4 5 6 7 8 9 10-ML-06 05 04 03 02 01 00

The Line

by Stacey Sparks

Lea and Mara were not getting along.

"I don't like sharing a room with you anymore," said Lea.

"I don't like sharing one with you!" answered Mara.

So Lea took a piece of white chalk and drew a line down the center of the floor. Then Lea sat on her bed and Mara sat on hers.

After a while, Lea got bored. She wanted to listen to the radio, but it was on Mara's side of the room.

"Mara, could you turn on the radio?" she asked.

"No," said Mara. "I'm resting."

"Well, could you at least give me my library book?"

"Sorry," said Mara. "I'm busy." Then she sneezed. "Help!" she said. "I need a tissue!"

"Too bad they're on my side of the room!" said Lea.

"Please!" begged Mara.

Lea gave in. She threw a tissue to Mara. Mara blew her nose. Then Mara decided to be nice too. She tossed Lea's book across the line.

All afternoon they had to pass things back and forth.

That night, both girls went up to bed.

"Could you turn on the light?" asked Mara.

"Could you hand me my pj's?" asked Lea.

"Oh no. What about our hair?" asked Mara.

GO ON

Every night, the girls sat on Mara's bed and braided each other's hair.

"I guess you could stand on your side, and I could stand on mine," said Lea.

They tried. But there was no place to set the brush down. Lea tried holding it in her teeth. Then she started to <u>chuckle</u>. The brush fell to the floor. Mara started to laugh too.

"This is silly!" they both said at the same time.

"Not sharing is such hard work," groaned Lea.

So together they erased the white line.

Questions 1–10. Fill in the circle beside the best answer to each question, or write your answer on the lines.

1. How do Lea and Mara feel at the beginning of the story?

____

____

____

____

2. Where does this story take place?
Ⓐ at school
Ⓑ in the girls' bedroom
Ⓒ in the kitchen

3. Lea drew a line on the floor to
Ⓐ help Mara get to the door.
Ⓑ play a game with Mara.
Ⓒ divide the room in half.

GO ON ▶

4. The story says, "Then she started to <u>chuckle</u>." What does <u>chuckle</u> mean?

  Ⓐ laugh

  Ⓑ cry

  Ⓒ yell

5. Which sentence best tells what this story is about?

  Ⓐ Two sisters get different rooms.

  Ⓑ Two sisters paint their room.

  Ⓒ Two sisters have trouble sharing a room.

6. When Lea wanted to listen to the radio, Mara was

  Ⓐ resting.

  Ⓑ brushing her hair.

  Ⓒ reading a book.

7. Why did the girls start sharing again?

____

____

GO ON

8. The story says that Lea drew a line on the <u>floor</u>. Which word has the same sounds as the <u>oor</u> in <u>floor</u>?

   Ⓐ her

   Ⓑ more

   Ⓒ turn

9. The story says, "Mara <u>blew</u> her nose." Which word has the same sound as the <u>ew</u> in <u>blew</u>?

   Ⓐ too

   Ⓑ brown

   Ⓒ cream

10. Which word best fits in the sentence?
Lea brushed __________ hair.

   Ⓐ Maras

   Ⓑ Mara

   Ⓒ Mara's

STOP

Who Cut Them Down?

by Stacey Sparks

Squirrel carried twigs up the tree. She wove them into a strong nest. "Good," she said. "I can raise my babies in that nest."

She went off to find some leaves and grass. She wanted the nest to be soft and warm. When she came back, she looked around. Where was the tree? It was gone!

She ran closer. The tree was lying on the ground. Something had cut right through it. Bits of her nest lay on the ground beside it.

So Squirrel found another tree. Up and down she <u>rushed</u>, making another nest. Again she ran off to find soft leaves. When she returned, the second tree lay on the ground.

There was no time to fuss. Squirrel's babies would be born soon. They would need a nest. She found a third tree.

Just then Mouse came along. Squirrel told Mouse the whole story. Mouse had an idea.

"Build another nest. Then go away. I will stay and watch. I am so small, I can hide in the grass. I will find out who is cutting down the trees."

Squirrel made the finest nest of all. Then she dashed off. Mouse hid in the grass and waited.

Along came a beaver. He started to chew on the tree with his great big teeth.

"Stop!" squeaked Mouse.

The beaver jumped. "What's wrong?"

"You keep cutting down the trees where Squirrel has built her nest. That's mean," scolded Mouse.

Just then, Squirrel came back. She dropped the leaves from her mouth. Then she started to scold too.

"I'm sorry," said the beaver. "I was cutting down trees to make a home for *my* babies. I didn't know there were nests in them. I won't cut down this tree. Your nest is safe."

"Thank you," said Squirrel.

Questions 11–20. Fill in the circle beside the best answer to each question, or write your answer on the lines.

11. Why was Squirrel making a nest?
    - Ⓐ She was cold.
    - Ⓑ She wanted a place to hide.
    - Ⓒ She needed a home for her babies.

12. Where does this story take place?
    - Ⓐ in the woods
    - Ⓑ on a beach
    - Ⓒ in a zoo

13. How did Squirrel lose her first two nests?

____

____

____

14. Who was better at hiding, Squirrel or Mouse? Tell why.

____

____

____

GO ON ▶

I5. The story says, "Up and down she <u>rushed</u>, making another nest." What does <u>rushed</u> mean?

(A) worried

(B) ran

(C) looked

I6. Name one way that Beaver and Squirrel are alike.

____

____

I7. How did Beaver feel when Squirrel and Mouse scolded her?

(A) sorry

(B) angry

(C) pleased

18. The story says, "So Squirrel <u>found</u> another tree." Which word has the same sound as the <u>ou</u> in <u>found</u>?

Ⓐ you

Ⓑ would

Ⓒ down

19. Squirrel said, "I can r<u>ai</u>se my babies." Which word has the same sound as the underlined letter in r<u>ai</u>se?

Ⓐ grass

Ⓑ lazy

Ⓒ safe

20. Think about the two stories you have read: "The Line" and "Who Cut Them Down?" What lesson about getting along together do both stories teach?

____

____

____

____

PART 2: RESPONDING TO LITERATURE

In these two stories, you have read about characters who learned to work together.

Think of a time when you learned to do something better by working with another person. Write a paragraph telling what happened to you and what you learned. Your paragraph should have at least four sentences. Tell what happened in the right time order.

Write your paragraph for a family member to read. When you finish, check your work.

GO ON

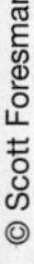

Ties Through Time

Unit 4 Benchmark Test

Name ______________________________

Date ______________________________

Scott Foresman
Reading
Grade 2

Editorial Offices
Glenview, Illinois • New York, New York

Sales Offices
Reading, Massachusetts • Duluth, Georgia • Glenview, Illinois
Carrollton, Texas • Menlo Park, California

ISBN 0-673-62371-8

2 3 4 5 6 7 8 9 10-ML-06 05 04 03 02 01 00

Marching On

by Joanna Evans

It was time for the Founder's Day Parade in Sharon's hometown. Sharon's whole class was going to march in the parade, which was held every year. Sharon didn't want to be left out.

Sharon and the other kids picked up their signs. Then they got into lines. When the whistle blew, they started to march.

The parade began at the school, went past the fire house, and ended at the library. Then the children sat on the grass by the library. Their teacher, Mr. Day, stood on the steps.

"Oh, no," Sharon thought. "This will be another long speech."

Sharon heard bits of the speech. She heard that the person who <u>founded</u> the town was Joshua Jones. He was a farmer long ago, and his life was hard.

Now Sharon wanted to hear more.

"He lived in a small cabin," Mr. Day said. "His seven children all slept in the same room. They never had much to eat. They all worked many hours on the farm."

"That must have been hard," Sharon thought.

"When Joshua Jones was an old man," Mr. Day said, "he let people put a school on his land. He let people build a town hall on his land, and a library— this library. You are all sitting on Joshua Jones's farm."

Sharon looked around. It was nice to think about this land being so important.

"Joshua Jones never asked for money," Mr. Day said. "He loved this place and the people in it. That's why we have a town today."

"Wow," Sharon thought. "What a special person! We should do something to remember him. We should all get together. We should—"

She stopped and smiled.

"We should have a parade," she said.

Questions 1–10. Fill in the circle beside the best answer to each question, or write your answer on the lines.

1. What happened at the beginning of the story?
   - Ⓐ Sharon went to the fire house.
   - Ⓑ Sharon sat down on the grass.
   - Ⓒ Sharon got ready to march in the parade.

2. What did Sharon and the other kids do just after they picked up their signs?

   ____

   -

   ____

   ____

   -

   ____

3. The story says that Joshua Jones <u>founded</u> the town. What does <u>founded</u> mean?
   - Ⓐ left
   - Ⓑ liked
   - Ⓒ started

GO ON ➡

4. What made Sharon change her mind and start
to like Mr. Day's speech?
  (A) talking with her friends
  (B) hearing about Joshua Jones
  (C) marching in the parade

5. How are the school, the fire house, and the
library alike?
  (A) They are places the parade passed.
  (B) They are places where people borrow
       books.
  (C) They are places Joshua Jones built.

6. Why did Joshua Jones give his land to the town?

____

- -

____

____

- -

____

7. Why did Sharon smile at the end of the story?
  (A) She realized that people were already
       having parades to remember Mr. Jones.
  (B) Mr. Day told a funny joke in his speech.
  (C) She was glad that the parade and the
       speech were finally over.

8. The story says that the parade was held every year. Which word has the same sounds as the ear in year?

(A) deer

(B) door

(C) dare

9. Sharon thought Mr. Day would make a long speech. Which word has the same sound as the ough in thought?

(A) should

(B) hall

(C) town

10. Sharon's whole class was going to march. Which word begins with the same sound as whole?

(A) old

(B) land

(C) him

STOP

Deer Hunter and White Corn Maiden
A Tewa Folktale

retold by Joanna Evans

A long time ago, Deer Hunter was a great hunter. White Corn Maiden made the best pottery and dresses in the village. They met one day and fell in love. Before long, they got married. They were very happy.

For weeks they spent so much time together that Deer Hunter forgot about hunting. The village began to run out of food. White Corn Maiden forgot about making pots and dresses. The village began to run out of pots and dresses.

Things got so bad that the village leaders talked to Deer Hunter and White Corn Maiden. "Young people in our village have always done the hunting," they said. "Young people in our village have always made pots and dresses. You are not doing your part. We are very worried."

Deer Hunter and White Corn Maiden did not care. They still spent all their time together.

One day, a man walked into the village. He was tall and strong, and he spoke in a deep voice.

"Deer Hunter and White Corn Maiden," he said, "come to me."

Deer Hunter and White Corn Maiden were afraid. For once, they did what they were told. They went to him.

"Deer Hunter and White Corn Maiden," the man said, "you have not followed our people's traditions. You have not done your part. So you must go high up in the sky."

He waved his hand. Deer Hunter and White Corn Maiden <u>disappeared</u>.

From that day on, two new stars could be seen at night. They were close together, and one chased the other across the sky.

When the people of the village look up at the evening sky, they remember that it is important to do their part.

Questions 11–20. Fill in the circle beside the best answer to each question, or write your answer on the lines.

11. What did Deer Hunter and White Corn Maiden
    do first in this story?

    ____

    ____

    ____

12. Why did Deer Hunter and White Corn Maiden
    stop hunting and making pots?
    (A) They were not strong.
    (B) They left the village.
    (C) They spent all their time together.

13. Where does this story take place?

    ____

    ____

    ____

GO ON ➤

14. The story says, "Deer Hunter and White Corn Maiden <u>disappeared</u>." What does <u>disappeared</u> mean?

   Ⓐ went hunting

   Ⓑ went away suddenly

   Ⓒ walked slowly

15. What happened to Deer Hunter and White Corn Maiden at the end of the story?

   Ⓐ They went back to doing their jobs.

   Ⓑ They became stars in the sky.

   Ⓒ They got married.

16. Which job was **not** done by young people in the village?

   Ⓐ building houses

   Ⓑ hunting

   Ⓒ making pots and dresses

GO ON ▶

17. Why were the village leaders worried about
Deer Hunter and White Corn Maiden? Give one
reason.

____

____

____

____

18. Which word best fits in the sentence below?
White Corn Maiden's pots were the _________ of
all.
Ⓐ fine
Ⓑ finer
Ⓒ finest

GO ON

19. Which word means the same as the underlined
words?
When they saw the tall man, Deer Hunter and
White Corn Maiden were <u>full of fear</u>.
Ⓐ fearful
Ⓑ fear
Ⓒ fearly

20. Think about the two stories you have read:
"Marching On" and "Deer Hunter and White
Corn Maiden." Both stories show that
Ⓐ farmers can start towns.
Ⓑ people are running out of food.
Ⓒ traditions are important.

STOP

PART 2: RESPONDING TO LITERATURE

Think about the characters in these two stories:
Sharon in "Marching On" and Deer Hunter and
White Corn Maiden in the folktale. What happened
to each character? How do you think each one felt?

Choose a character—Sharon, Deer Hunter, or
White Corn Maiden. Pretend to be that character,
and write a journal entry of four to six sentences.
Tell about what happened to you in the story. Be
sure your entry has a beginning, middle, and end.

Write your journal entry for a friend to read. When
you finish, check your work.

STOP

All Aboard!

Name ______________________________

Date ______________________________

Scott Foresman

Reading

Grade 2

Editorial Offices
Glenview, Illinois • New York, New York

Sales Offices
Reading, Massachusetts • Duluth, Georgia • Glenview, Illinois
Carrollton, Texas • Menlo Park, California

ISBN 0-673-62372-6

2 3 4 5 6 7 8 9 10-ML-06 05 04 03 02 01 00

Friends Far from Home

by Theo Trudelle

Zina and her mom were on their way to visit Grandma in Pennsylvania. They had been driving for a long time. Zina was very hot. She was also tired of just sitting. "How much longer?" she asked.

Her mom didn't answer. "What's the matter?" asked Zina.

"Something is wrong with the car," said Mom.

Zina's mom stopped the car and got out. Zina followed her, watching as she raised the car's hood. Steam suddenly came pouring out. "Oh, no," said Mom.

"Wow!" cried Zina. "Look at that!"

"Be careful," said Mom, "it's hot."

Zina's mom looked around. There were no houses or people nearby. "I think we'll have to walk," she said. She took Zina's hand. "Come on, let's go find help."

They walked and walked. Finally they spotted a farm up ahead. Just then they heard a clip-clop, clip-clop sound. A young Amish boy was driving a horse-drawn <u>buggy</u>. He pulled on the reins and stopped next to them. Samuel gave them a ride the rest of the way to his family's farm.

At the farm, Zina's mom asked for a jug of water. "I think that's all I'll need to fix the car," she said. Then she and Samuel rode in the buggy back to the car. Zina stayed at the farm with Samuel's family.

At first Zina felt a bit out of place. The Amish house was very plain. There was no TV, no radio, not even a telephone. Zina was very surprised.

Also, Samuel's sisters did not dress like Zina. They wore long dresses and white caps on their heads. Zina forgot about all that, though, when the girls asked if she wanted to play tag. Soon, they all were laughing and playing.

"They're just like me," thought Zina. She couldn't wait to tell her mom.

Questions 1– 10. Fill in the circle beside the best answer to each question, or write your answer on the lines.

1. Where were Zina and her mom going?

____

____

____

2. What was Mom worried about at the beginning of the story?
   Ⓐ She was getting tired from driving so long.
   Ⓑ Something was wrong with the car.
   Ⓒ Zina was not having fun.

3. The story says that Samuel was in a horse-drawn <u>buggy</u>. What is a <u>buggy</u>?
   Ⓐ a wagon
   Ⓑ a car
   Ⓒ a farmhouse

4. What was making the clip-clop sound that Zina and her mom heard?
   Ⓐ a car
   Ⓑ a drum
   Ⓒ a horse

5. Which word best describes Samuel?

    (A) mean

    (B) helpful

    (C) afraid

6. Samuel's sisters were different from Zina because

    (A) their clothes were not like hers.

    (B) they lived on a farm.

    (C) they were wearing boys' clothes.

7. What did Zina learn from playing tag with the Amish children? Tell one thing she learned.

____

- -

____

- -

____

GO ON ▶

8. Which word best completes the sentence?
Zina didn't see many _________.
(A) house
(B) houses
(C) house's

9. In the story, Samuel pulled on the <u>reins</u>. Which word has the same sound as the <u>ei</u> in <u>reins</u>?
(A) cried
(B) them
(C) day

10. Which word best completes the sentence?
The girls wore long _________.
(A) dresses
(B) dress's
(C) dress

STOP

Traveling Back in Time

by Theo Trudelle

These days you can find almost anything you need at a store. What if that were suddenly no longer true? What would happen then?

If you traveled back in time to a hundred years ago in America, most people lived on farms. In many places, there were no stores. Almost everything people needed, they made themselves.

Back then, people had to know how to raise animals, grow their own food, and make their own clothes. Because there was so much work to be done, children had to help. Boys mostly worked outside, plowing the fields, planting crops, and chopping wood. Girls had to make clothes and <u>prepare</u> food. They also helped make butter, soap, and candles.

Making butter was one job that even very young children could do. First, they milked the cows. Then they brought the fresh milk into the house. They let the milk sit until the cream rose to the top. Then they poured the cream into a butter churn.

Butter Churn

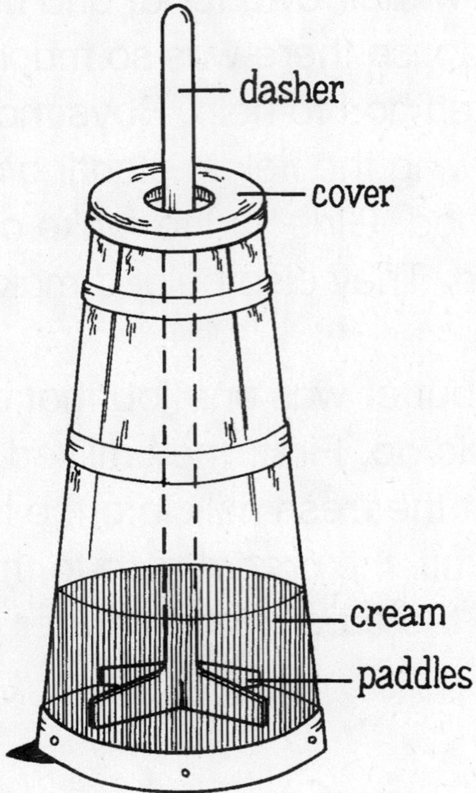

The churn was a tall wooden bucket. It had a long pole that was pumped up and down to make butter. Churning the butter was often the children's job. It wasn't hard to do, but it was very tiring. To help make the time pass more quickly, the children often sang as they worked.

Later, everyone got to eat the butter. The children must have felt proud. They had helped make something their family needed.

GO ON ➤

Questions 11–20. Fill in the circle beside the best answer to each question, or write your answer on the lines.

11. What is this selection mostly about?
- Ⓐ going to the store
- Ⓑ how to raise animals on a farm
- Ⓒ what life was like in America long ago

12. Which job was **not** done by boys on the farm?
- Ⓐ making clothes
- Ⓑ chopping wood
- Ⓒ plowing the fields

13. According to the selection, what did the children do after they milked the cows?
- Ⓐ They played with their friends.
- Ⓑ They brought the milk into the house.
- Ⓒ They drank the milk.

14. The selection says that girls had to <u>prepare</u> food. What does <u>prepare</u> mean?
- Ⓐ make ready
- Ⓑ buy at a store
- Ⓒ throw away

GO ON ➡

15. Look at the picture of a butter churn on page 8.
What is the long pole called?

____

- -

____

- -

____

16. Tell one way that life in America a hundred years
ago was different from what life is like today.

____

- -

____

- -

____

17. Which sentence is **not** a fact?
Ⓐ "The churn was a tall wooden bucket."
Ⓑ "First, they milked the cows."
Ⓒ "The children must have felt proud."

18. Most <u>young</u> children had to work. Which word has the same sound as the <u>ou</u> in <u>young</u>?

Ⓐ much

Ⓑ soap

Ⓒ house

19. Which word has the same sound as the <u>ue</u> in <u>true</u>?

Ⓐ but

Ⓑ proud

Ⓒ you

20. Think about the Amish children you read about in "Friends Far from Home." Tell one way they were like the children in "Traveling Back in Time."

STOP

PART 2: RESPONSING TO LITERATURE

The two selections you have read are about other places or other times. What did you learn from traveling with Zina and her mom in "Friends Far from Home," or from "Traveling Back in Time"?

Choose the selection you liked better. Write a paragraph to explain what you learned from reading the selection. Use words such as *first* and *next* to connect ideas.

Write your paragraph for a friend to read. When you finish, check your work.

GO ON ▶

STOP

Just Imagine!

Unit 6 Benchmark Test

Name ______________________________

Date ______________________________

Scott Foresman

Reading

Grade 2

Editorial Offices
Glenview, Illinois • New York, New York

Sales Offices
Reading, Massachusetts • Duluth, Georgia • Glenview, Illinois
Carrollton, Texas • Menlo Park, California

ISBN 0-673-62373-4

2 3 4 5 6 7 8 9 10-ML-06 05 04 03 02 01 00

A Clean Sweep

by Joanna Evans

Characters:
    Emma, a seven-year-old girl
    Emma's mother

Setting: Emma's room. It is a mess. Emma is playing with a toy school bus. Emma's mother enters.

EMMA'S MOTHER: Oh my! Just look at this mess! If you want to play softball this afternoon, you'll have to clean up this room. *(She leaves.)*

EMMA: I hate cleaning up my room. It's never any fun. I wish I could go outside and play softball right now. *(She sits on the floor and <u>frowns</u>.)* Well, it's not getting clean while I sit here. What can I do to make this more fun?

(Emma sits and thinks for a moment. Then she looks at the clock on her wall.)

EMMA: I know! If I can't play on a softball team, I'll play on a room-cleaning team! That way, I'll have lots of help.

(Emma picks up a wool sweater from a pile of clothes on a chair.)

EMMA: I'm the pitcher, and I'll throw the sweater-ball to the catcher by the dresser.

(Emma throws the sweater into a drawer and then runs over to the dresser.)

EMMA: Great throw! Strike one!

(She folds the sweater and puts it away. Then she picks up a toy.)

EMMA: Oh, no! Someone is running to first base!

(She dashes over to the toy box and puts the toy inside.)

EMMA: You're out! The first baseman tagged the runner with the ball!

(The curtain comes down for a moment. When it rises, the room is clean. Emma's mother enters.)

EMMA'S MOTHER: Why, Emma! You cleaned up your whole room! Now you may go play softball.

EMMA: *(smiles)* Thanks, Mom! I got my whole team to help me clean up!

(Emma runs out the door. Her mother smiles and shakes her head.)

(Curtain)

GO ON

Questions 1– 10. Fill in the circle beside the best answer to each question, or write your answer on the lines.

1. What does Emma have to do before she can play softball?

____

____

____

2. Emma pretends to be a
Ⓐ bus driver.
Ⓑ softball player.
Ⓒ toy maker.

3. The play says, "She sits on the floor and frowns." What does <u>frowns</u> mean?
Ⓐ looks unhappy or upset
Ⓑ plays catch with a ball
Ⓒ crosses her legs

4. Where does this play take place?

____

____

GO ON ➤

5. What lesson can be learned from this play?
  (A) Always work before you play.
  (B) Work is easier if you make it fun.
  (C) Softball is a fun game.

6. Is this a realistic story or a fantasy? Give one reason why you think so.

____

____

____

____

7. Why do you think Emma smiles at the end of the play?
  (A) She knows her mother will finish cleaning the room.
  (B) She cleaned her room and had fun at the same time.
  (C) She is going to tell her friends how to play softball.

GO ON ▶

8. At the end of the play, how did Emma's mother feel when she saw Emma's room?

(A) angry

(B) sad

(C) surprised

9. Emma plays with a toy <u>school</u> bus. Which word begins with the same sounds as <u>school</u>?

(A) sat

(B) skate

(C) chop

10. Clothes are piled on a <u>chair</u>. Which word has the same sounds as the <u>air</u> in <u>chair</u>?

(A) care

(B) bar

(C) here

STOP

The Oddball Race

by Joanna Evans

At the Fourth of July picnic, people ate hot dogs and flew kites. People sang and listened to music. People talked and laughed.

They also entered a lot of contests. There was a three-legged race and a sack hop. There was a crawling race. There was a pie-baking contest, a pie-eating contest, and a pie-throwing contest.

LaMar ignored them. He stood off to one side, quietly flying his big red kite. He looked over at his friends. They were flying kites too. The wind was blowing hard, and the kites <u>soared</u> easily.

The only contest LaMar wanted to enter was the Oddball Race. People in the race had to get across a wide patch of grass—without touching the ground with their feet. The first one to get across without touching the ground would be the winner. The prize was a new bike.

No bikes or skateboards were allowed. Every year, people were carried across. They jumped across on pogo sticks. They rolled across in barrels.

This year, LaMar had a plan. As everyone lined up at one end of the field, LaMar moved slowly toward them. Then, just as the starting horn sounded, he ran to the line. So did his friends, each one flying a kite. LaMar grabbed all the kite strings, tugged hard, and jumped into the air.

He sailed like a leaf over everyone's heads, and he tumbled to a stop just across the finish line. He was there long before anyone else. As the judge named him the winner, he stood up and smiled. Then he waved to the friends who had helped.

Whenever his friends visited him after that, he always invited them to ride his new bike.

Questions 11–20. Fill in the circle beside the best answer to each question, or write your answer on the lines.

11. What happened just as the Oddball Race started?
    (A) The other children let LaMar use all the kites.
    (B) LaMar and his friends made a plan.
    (C) LaMar's friends started flying kites.

12. How did LaMar get a new bike?

    ____
    -
    ____

    ____
    -
    ____

13. The story says, "The wind was blowing hard, and the kites <u>soared</u> easily." What does <u>soared</u> mean?
    (A) sat still
    (B) flew high
    (C) were found

GO ON ➡

14. Which is a big idea of this story?

    Ⓐ New ways sometimes work better than old ways.

    Ⓑ Contests are fun to enter.

    Ⓒ Flying kites is an exciting sport.

15. What was needed for LaMar's plan to work?

    Ⓐ The other people needed to get a late start.

    Ⓑ The race had to start on time.

    Ⓒ The wind had to be blowing in the right direction.

16. Which part of this story probably did **not** really happen?

    Ⓐ People ate hot dogs and flew kites.

    Ⓑ The wind was blowing hard.

    Ⓒ LaMar flew up in the air.

17. The story says that people talked and lau<u>gh</u>ed. Which word has the same sound as the underlined letters in lau<u>gh</u>ed?

    Ⓐ phone

    Ⓑ huge

    Ⓒ game

18. In the story, people listened to music. Which word has the same sound as the underlined letter in m<u>u</u>sic?

Ⓐ cupful

Ⓑ cuter

Ⓒ mother

19. Which word best fits in the sentence below? The wind blew the _________ on the trees.

Ⓐ leaf

Ⓑ leafes

Ⓒ leaves

20. Think of the two characters you have read about, Emma in "A Clean Sweep" and LaMar in "The Oddball Race." Name one way they are alike.

____

____

____

____

____

PART 2: RESPONDING TO LITERATURE

Think about what Emma and LaMar did in these two selections, "A Clean Sweep" and "The Oddball Race." Which person do you think had a better idea?

Choose one of the two characters, Emma or LaMar. Write a friendly letter to that person. Tell the person what you thought of his or her idea. Include details from the play or story. Your friendly letter should be four to six sentences long. Be sure to use correct letter form. When you finish, check your work.

GO ON ▶

End-of-Year Benchmark Test

Name _______________________________

Date _______________________________

Scott Foresman
Reading
Grade 2

Acknowledgments:
"Linda's Invention" by Dina Anastasio from RAINBOW SHOWER. Copyright © 1983 by Scott, Foresman and Company.

Editorial Offices
Glenview, Illinois • New York, New York

Sales Offices
Reading, Massachusetts • Duluth, Georgia • Glenview, Illinois
Carrollton, Texas • Menlo Park, California

ISBN 0-673-62399-8

2 3 4 5 6 7 8 9 10-ML-06 05 04 03 02 01 00

Linda's Invention

by Dina Anastasio

It was a hot day in the city. Linda and her friends were sitting on the <u>stoop</u> in front of an apartment building.

After a while Linda got up, walked to the curb, and looked down.

"This city is a mess," she said. "You can hardly see the street anymore. Before long we won't be able to find the cars or the people or even the buildings. This city is really a mess!"

Linda's friends nodded, but said nothing.

"Don't you *care?*" Linda asked.

Again, Linda's friends said nothing.

End-of-Year Benchmark Test   **1**

"Well, I care," Linda said. "And I'm going to do something about it. I'm going to invent something that will clean up every piece of garbage on the street."

"Sure," said Luis, yawning.

"It's impossible," said Ann without looking up.

"Great idea," said Diane, trying hard not to laugh.

Linda's friends had heard it all before. Linda was *always* going to invent something.

When it was hot, Linda was going to invent a machine that would keep her cool.

When she was sad, Linda was going to invent a machine that would hug her and make her laugh.

When she had nothing to do, Linda was going to invent her very own roller coaster.

One day Linda was going to invent a fire hose that sprayed red-and-white water.

And the next day she was going to invent a robot that sang "Linda is never wrong, Linda is never wrong."

But Linda never invented anything.

"All right," said Linda. "You just wait!" And she ran into the apartment building.

Linda did not come out to play the next day, or the day after that.

"Maybe she's sick," said Luis.

"Maybe she went to her uncle's," said Ann.

"Maybe she's inventing a machine to clean up the streets," said Diane. Then everyone laughed. They all knew that Linda would never invent anything.

Early the next morning Linda came out of the building. She was carrying a big box. The top of the box had a large hole cut out of it. Above the hole were written the words "THE GARBAGE GAME." Under the hole were the words "TOSS IT IN HERE AND WIN!"

Linda put the box on the sidewalk next to the street. Then she walked back to the stoop and sat down next to her friends.

"What's that?" asked Luis.

"It's my invention," Linda said.

Linda's friends looked at the box and laughed.

"That's silly," said Ann. "How's that going to clean up our street?"

"Just wait," said Linda.

"We'll have to wait for months," laughed Diane.

Linda and her friends sat on the stoop and waited.

At 10 o'clock Luis went upstairs to get an apple. After he had finished eating it, he tossed it into the box.

"That's really a silly game," he said. "It's much too easy. Anybody can hit that hole."

Linda didn't say anything.

At 11 a piece of paper floated by. Diane picked it up and tossed it into the box.

"The hole's too big," she said. "It's impossible to miss."

Linda didn't say anything.

At 12 a young boy rode by on his bike. He was peeling a banana. When he saw the box, he stopped and threw the peel into it. Then he said, "What do I win?"

GO ON

"Look at the clean sidewalk," said Linda.

The boy looked. Then he shrugged and got back on his bike. As he turned the corner, he said, "That's a very silly game."

The next four people who came by tossed their garbage into the box.

Linda didn't say anything.

But Luis did. "I see," he said. "The hole is supposed to be big. That way no one can miss."

Linda smiled.

"The sidewalk *is* pretty clean," said Ann.

Linda smiled again.

"Not a bad invention," said Diane.

Linda kept right on smiling.

No one said anything for a long time. They were looking at the sidewalk. Then Luis leaned back and said, "You know, it's nice."

"Yes," Linda said. "It's very nice."

GO ON

Questions 1–15. Fill in the circle beside the best answer to each question, or write your answer on the lines.

1. Where does this story take place?

____

____

____

2. What kind of person is Linda?
- Ⓐ silly
- Ⓑ clever
- Ⓒ scary

3. The story says, "Linda and her friends were sitting on the <u>stoop</u> in front of an apartment building." What is a <u>stoop</u>?
- Ⓐ a short set of stairs
- Ⓑ a piece of garbage
- Ⓒ a group of apartments

4. What happened last in this story?
- Ⓐ Linda invented the garbage game.
- Ⓑ People tossed their garbage into a box.
- Ⓒ Linda noticed the street was a mess.

GO ON

5. What does Diane think of Linda's invention at the end of the story?

____

- -

____

____

- -

____

6. The prize for playing the garbage game is a
- Ⓐ piece of fruit.
- Ⓑ toy.
- Ⓒ clean sidewalk.

7. The next time Linda says she is going to invent something, what will most likely happen?
- Ⓐ Her friends will believe her.
- Ⓑ A robot will say, "Linda is never wrong."
- Ⓒ She will not invent anything.

8. Which is a big idea of this story?
- Ⓐ Young people cannot invent things by themselves.
- Ⓑ When lots of people help, cleaning up is fun and easy.
- Ⓒ People do not like to clean up a big mess.

9. At the beginning of the story, how was Linda different from her friends in the way she felt about the city?

____

____

____

10. Linda's friends were right to think she would not invent a machine to clean the streets because she
   Ⓐ had never invented anything before.
   Ⓑ said she was going to visit her uncle.
   Ⓒ never had any ideas for inventions.

11. Linda said, "You just <u>wait</u>!" Which word has the same sound as the <u>ai</u> in <u>wait</u>?
   Ⓐ star
   Ⓑ stack
   Ⓒ stay

12. The top of the box had a <u>large</u> hole in it. Which word has the same sounds as the <u>ar</u> in <u>large</u>?

Ⓐ care

Ⓑ tar

Ⓒ bare

13. The robot was going to say, "Linda is never <u>wrong</u>." Which word begins with the same sound as <u>wrong</u>?

Ⓐ wide

Ⓑ when

Ⓒ ride

14. Everyone la<u>ugh</u>ed. Which word has the same sound as the underlined letters in la<u>ugh</u>ed?

Ⓐ go

Ⓑ hot

Ⓒ off

GO ON ▶

15. Which is a compound word?
- (A) doesn't
- (B) sidewalk
- (C) beautiful

Questions 16– 17. Read each sentence. Find the word that best completes the sentence.

16. Linda answered the _________ question.
- (A) boys
- (B) boy
- (C) boy's

17. The street was _________ now than it used to be.
- (A) cleaner
- (B) cleanest
- (C) clean

STOP

About Dr. Seuss

by Elise C. Williams

Dr. Seuss wrote 47 books for children of all ages. His books were loved by people all over the world. Children loved his book *Green Eggs and Ham* so much that they used to send Dr. Seuss green eggs and ham in the mail! The people at the post office didn't like that very much. But Dr. Seuss loved to get mail every day. He loved reading the letters he got from children.

In their letters, children asked Dr. Seuss questions about his books. Many children asked where he got all his funny ideas. His answer was that he wasn't really sure. Those ideas just seemed to pop into his mind.

GO ON

What kind of man was Dr. Seuss? He was shy.
He did not like crowds of people. He lived in a pink
house at the top of a hill. He had a sign that said
"Beware of the Cat." Since Dr. Seuss didn't have a
cat, the sign could have been about his storybook
character, the Cat in the Hat.

Dr. Seuss always said he could not draw real
animals. So he drew strange and wonderful
<u>creatures</u> like the Cat in the Hat, the Grinch, and
Horton the elephant. He had boxes of colored
pencils all over his desk. He used the pencils to
draw his silly characters.

This well-loved author did not write all of his books sitting at his desk. His favorite book, *The Lorax,* was written while he was sitting by a pool on vacation. It was about a green animal who speaks for the trees that are being cut down. Dr. Seuss believed that people need to take care of the trees and the rest of the Earth.

Many of the books Dr. Seuss wrote had strange creatures who did things that were funny. *The Cat in the Hat* is a book about a talking cat. This cat wears a tall, red-and-white striped hat. The Cat in the Hat visits two children on a rainy day and does all kinds of silly tricks. But his tricks make a big mess.

In the book *Green Eggs and Ham*, Dr. Seuss wrote about a character named Sam-I-Am. Sam-I-Am tries to get his friend to eat green eggs and ham. But his friend doesn't want to eat eggs and ham that are green. Sam-I-Am doesn't give up though.

   Just like his character Sam-I-Am, Dr. Seuss
never gave up. He said that writing books was hard
work. Sometimes it would take two or three years to
write one. After he wrote a book, he would make
lots of changes. He would keep changing things to
make the book better. He wanted his books to be
good so people would like them.

   Dr. Seuss wanted people to know how much
fun reading could be. He worked hard every day to
write stories that children and grown-ups would
enjoy again and again. He thought that knowing
how to read was important, so he wrote many
books to help children learn to read. Best of all, his
books made children laugh while they learned.
Some books, like *Green Eggs and Ham*, made Dr.
Seuss laugh too.

18. What is this selection mostly about?
- Ⓐ green eggs and ham
- Ⓑ Dr. Seuss
- Ⓒ books

19. The author wrote this selection to
- Ⓐ make readers laugh.
- Ⓑ tell how to draw pictures.
- Ⓒ give information about Dr. Seuss.

20. The selection says that Dr. Seuss drew strange and wonderful <u>creatures</u>. The creatures he drew were
- Ⓐ stories.
- Ⓑ made-up animals.
- Ⓒ children.

GO ON ▶

21. Why did Dr. Seuss spend so much time on each of his books?

____

- -

____

- -

____

22. What did Dr. Seuss look like? Write a sentence to describe him.

____

- -

____

- -

____

23. Which sentence gives an opinion?

(A) *The Lorax* was written while Dr. Seuss was sitting by a pool.

(B) It was about a green animal who speaks for the trees.

(C) Writing books was hard work.

24. Children seem to love books by Dr. Seuss.
Name one detail you have read in the selection
that shows this.

____

- -

____

- -

____

25. What does the author of this selection think is
the best thing about books by Dr. Seuss?
- Ⓐ They make children laugh while they learn.
- Ⓑ Grown-ups enjoy reading them.
- Ⓒ They are full of characters that are not real.

26. Think about "Linda's Invention" and "About Dr.
Seuss." How was Linda like Dr. Seuss?
- Ⓐ She was shy.
- Ⓑ She liked to think up new ideas.
- Ⓒ She wanted everything to be very neat.

27. Both Linda and Dr. Seuss believed that people
should
- Ⓐ live in pink houses.
- Ⓑ read about make-believe animals.
- Ⓒ help take care of the world around them.

GO ON ▶

End-of-Year Benchmark Test **17**

28. The selection says, "The si<u>gn</u> could have been about his storybook character." Which word has the same sound as the underlined letters in si<u>gn</u>?

Ⓐ nose

Ⓑ geese

Ⓒ grow

29. Dr. Seuss said he could not draw <u>rea</u>l animals. Which word has the same sound as the <u>ea</u> in <u>rea</u>l?

Ⓐ ran

Ⓑ week

Ⓒ head

30. He drew silly <u>characters</u>. Which word has the same beginning sound as <u>characters</u>?

Ⓐ could

Ⓑ circle

Ⓒ chew

31. Dr. Seuss lived in a pink <u>house</u>. Which word has the same sound as the <u>ou</u> in <u>house</u> ?

Ⓐ not

Ⓑ know

Ⓒ now

32. He <u>thought</u> reading was important. Which word
has the same sound as the <u>ough</u> in <u>thought</u>?

(A) jaw

(B) join

(C) joke

Questions 33–35. Read each sentence. Find the word that best completes the sentence.

33. Dr. Seuss wrote many great __________.

(A) story's

(B) story

(C) stories

34. He liked __________ up new characters.

(A) making

(B) makeing

(C) makking

35. __________ save my copies of his books.

(A) Il'l

(B) I'll

(C) I'l

STOP

PART 2: RESPONDING TO LITERATURE

Think about the two selections you have read. Linda invented a game to help clean up her street. Many children wrote letters to Dr. Seuss. If a friend wanted to make up a game or write a letter, how should your friend do it?

Write a how-to paragraph that tells how to make "The Garbage Game" or how to write a letter. Your how-to paragraph should include three to five steps. Make sure it clearly explains how to do one of these things.

When you finish, check your work.

GO ON ▶

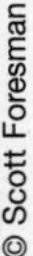

Answer Key

Unit 1 Benchmark Test

Part 1: Reading

Selection 1: "The Wedding Band"

1. A
2. A
3. on the road
4. B
5. outside of Pig's house
6. C
7. Wording may vary. Possible answers: Dog helped Pig by getting a band for his wedding. Dog helped Pig by doing whatever Pig needed.
8. C
9. B
10. B

Selection 2: "Jumping Jessica"

11. B
12. A
13. C
14. A
15. B
16. B
17. C
18. A
19. Possible answers: She loves to jump rope. She loves to chant or sing. She loves to jump rope with a friend. She invites Marie to join in with her and Claire.
20. Possible answers: In both stories, the friends help each other. In both stories, the friends have fun together.

Part 2: Responding to Literature

Scoring Guide: Story About Me

4 Exemplary
The student writes a story telling about something special that has happened to him or her. The story has a beginning, middle, and end. It has rich details that reveal the writer's feelings. The writing is on topic and appealing. Errors in grammar, usage, and mechanics are minimal and do not affect meaning.

3 Competent
The student writes a story telling about something special that has happened to him or her. The writer attempts a beginning, middle, and end. Details reveal the writer's feelings. The writing is on topic. It may include a few errors in grammar, usage, and mechanics, but they do not affect meaning.

2 Developing
The student writes a story telling about something special that has happened to him or her. The writer attempts to move the story to an end. A few details reveal the writer's feelings. The writing is generally on topic. It may include several errors in grammar, usage, and mechanics, which may affect meaning.

1 Emerging
The writer may attempt to write a story about himself or herself, but the writing shows little direction. The writer fails to reveal self through details. There is little or no development of topic. Errors in grammar, usage, and mechanics obscure meaning.

ANSWER KEY

Unit 2 Benchmark Test

Part 1: Reading

Selection 1: "Wonders of the Woods"

1. A
2. the maidenhair fern
3. B
4. C
5. Wording may vary. Possible answers: The water will be lower. The water will flow more slowly. The brook will be quieter.
6. C
7. A
8. B
9. C
10. A

Selection 2: "A Special Farm"

11. B
12. Wording may vary. Possible answers: It is a butterfly farm. The "farm animals" are butterflies. The farmers are children.
13. C
14. pupa
15. A
16. B
17. C
18. B
19. C
20. Wording may vary. Possible answers: They teach children about nature. They know a lot about nature. They help people.

Part 2: Responding to Literature

Scoring Guide: Descriptive Paragraph

4 Exemplary
The paragraph describes the nature trail or the butterfly farm. It uses vivid sensory words and images. Ideas are clear and elaborated with many strong details. Examples for the nature trail: Students might describe the size and shape of the ferns, the sound of the brook and the rushing water, the animal tracks, the inside of the rotting tree, the smell of rotting wood. Errors in grammar, usage, and mechanics are minimal and do not affect meaning.

3 Competent
The paragraph describes the nature trail or the butterfly farm. It includes sensory words and images. Ideas are reasonably clear and elaborated with three or more details. It may include a few errors in grammar, usage, and mechanics, but they do not affect meaning.

2 Developing
The paragraph describes the nature trail or the butterfly farm. It has some sensory words and/or images. Ideas may stray or lack clarity. Ideas are elaborated with two or more details. It may include several errors in grammar, usage, and mechanics, which may affect meaning.

1 Emerging
The paragraph does not describe the nature trail or the butterfly farm, or it does not accurately reflect the content of the passage. It has few or no sensory words or images. Ideas lack focus and clarity, and the paragraph lacks elaboration. Errors in grammar, usage, and mechanics obscure meaning.

ANSWER KEY

Unit 3 Benchmark Test

Part 1: Reading

Selection 1: "The Line"
1. Possible answers: They feel angry, grumpy, mad at each other, upset.
2. B
3. C
4. A
5. C
6. A
7. Wording may vary. Possible answers: They needed to braid each other's hair, or they realized that not sharing was hard work.
8. B
9. A
10. C

Selection 2: "Who Cut Them Down?"
11. C
12. A
13. Possible answers: They were ruined when the trees fell down. Beaver cut the trees down.
14. Mouse was better at hiding because he was smaller than Squirrel.
15. B
16. Possible answers: Both use trees to make homes for their babies; both are going to have babies.
17. A
18. C
19. B
20. Wording may vary. Possible answers: It is better to work together than to work against each other; not sharing is hard work.

Part 2: Responding to Literature

Scoring Guide: Narrative Paragraph

4 Exemplary
The paragraph tells about a time when the writer learned to do something better by working with another person. The paragraph has a strong beginning, middle, and end. It has good elaboration. Errors in grammar, usage, and mechanics are minimal and do not affect meaning.

3 Competent
The paragraph tells about a time when the writer learned to do something better by working with another person. The paragraph has a good beginning, middle, and end, and has adequate elaboration. It may include a few errors in grammar, usage, and mechanics, but they do not affect meaning.

2 Developing
The paragraph tells about a time when the writer learned to do something better by working with another person. The writer attempts a beginning, middle, and end. The paragraph could use more elaboration. It may include several errors in grammar, usage, and mechanics, which may affect meaning.

1 Emerging
The paragraph may tell about learning to work with another person, but it lacks progression from beginning to end. It has no transitions to show order of events and lacks elaboration. Errors in grammar, usage, and mechanics obscure meaning.

ANSWER KEY

Unit 4 Benchmark Test

Part 1: Reading

Selection 1: "Marching On"

1. C
2. They got into lines.
3. C
4. B
5. A
6. Wording may vary. Possible answer: He loved the place and the people.
7. A
8. A
9. B
10. C

Selection 2: "Deer Hunter and White Corn Maiden"

11. Wording may vary. Possible answer: They met and fell in love.
12. C
13. in a village, or in an Indian village
14. B
15. B
16. A
17. Wording may vary. Possible answers: They were not doing their part. The villagers were running out of food, pots, and clothes.
18. C
19. A
20. C

Part 2: Responding to Literature

Scoring Guide: Journal Entry

4 Exemplary
The journal entry is written from the point of view of one of the characters. It tells what happened to the character; has a strong beginning, middle, and end; and includes many rich details. For example, an entry for Sharon in "Marching On" might tell how she marched in the parade and became interested in Mr. Day's speech. She changed her mind about the importance of Founder's Day when she learned what a special person Joshua Jones was. Errors in grammar, usage, and mechanics are minimal and do not affect meaning.

3 Competent
The journal entry is written from the point of view of one of the characters. It tells what happened to the character and has a beginning, middle, and end, but it may not be particularly detailed. It may include a few errors in grammar, usage, and mechanics, but they do not affect meaning.

2 Developing
The journal entry tells what happened to one of the characters, but it may not be written from the character's point of view. The writer attempts a beginning, middle, and end. The entry may include several errors in grammar, usage, and mechanics, which may affect meaning.

1 Emerging
The writing does not tell what happened to one of the characters, does not accurately reflect the content of the story, or is not a journal entry. It lacks progression from beginning to end. Errors in grammar, usage, and mechanics obscure meaning.

Answer Key

Unit 5 Benchmark Test

Part 1: Reading

Selection 1: "Friends Far from Home"
1. to visit Grandma, or to Grandma's house
2. B
3. A
4. C
5. B
6. A
7. Wording may vary. Possible answers: She learned that the Amish children were just like her. She learned that all children like to play.
8. B
9. C
10. A

Selection 2: "Traveling Back in Time"
11. C
12. A
13. B
14. A
15. a dasher
16. Possible answers: People lived on farms; they made what they needed; there were no stores.
17. C
18. A
19. C
20. Possible answers: They lived on a farm; they worked on the farm; they did not have cars.

Part 2: Responding to Literature

Scoring Guide: Explanatory Paragraph

4 Exemplary
The paragraph explains what the writer learned from one of the selections. It has a strong statement of purpose and gives effective examples and explanations. Details are logically organized, and clue words are used. Example for "Traveling Back in Time": I learned that young children made the butter. First, they milked the cows. Next, they brought the milk into the house. Errors in grammar, usage, and mechanics are minimal and do not affect meaning.

3 Competent
The paragraph explains what the writer learned from one of the selections. It has a clear statement of purpose and gives adequate examples and explanations. Details are generally well organized. It may include a few errors in grammar, usage, and mechanics, but they do not affect meaning.

2 Developing
The paragraph explains what the writer learned from one of the selections. The writer attempts to state a purpose. The paragraph needs more examples and explanations. Organization of details may be weak. It may include several errors in grammar, usage, and mechanics, which may affect meaning.

1 Emerging
The paragraph does not explain what the writer learned from one of the selections or does not accurately reflect the content of the selection. Errors in grammar, usage, and mechanics obscure meaning.

ANSWER KEY

Unit 6 Benchmark Test

Part 1: Reading

Selection 1: "A Clean Sweep"

1. She has to clean up her room.
2. B
3. A
4. in Emma's room
5. B
6. Wording may vary. Possible answers: It is a realistic story because a girl in real life could do what Emma did. It is a fantasy because there was not really a whole softball team in Emma's room.
7. B
8. C
9. B
10. A

Selection 2: "The Oddball Race"

11. A
12. Wording may vary. Possible answer: It was his prize for winning the Oddball Race.
13. B
14. A
15. C
16. C
17. A
18. B
19. C
20. Wording may vary. Possible answer: They both use their imaginations to solve problems.

Part 2: Responding to Literature
Scoring Guide: Friendly Letter

4 Exemplary

The letter is written to either Emma or LaMar and engages the reader. It uses correct letter form, shows a clear sense of audience, and includes many details from the play or story. The writer tells what he or she thought about the character's idea. For example, a letter to LaMar might tell how clever his kite-flying idea was and how impressive it was that he and his friends worked together. Errors in grammar, usage, and mechanics are minimal and do not affect meaning.

3 Competent

The letter is written to either Emma or LaMar and engages the reader. It uses correct letter form and includes two or three details from the play or story. The writer tells what he or she thought about the character's idea. It may include a few errors in grammar, usage, and mechanics, but they do not affect meaning.

2 Developing

The letter is written to either Emma or LaMar and attempts to engage the reader. It follows the main parts of correct letter form and includes one or two details from the play or story. The writer tells what he or she thought about the character's idea. It may include several errors in grammar, usage, and mechanics, which may affect meaning.

1 Emerging

The piece is not a friendly letter, it is not addressed to Emma or LaMar, or it does not accurately reflect the content of the play or story. Errors in grammar, usage, and mechanics obscure meaning.

ANSWER KEY

End-of-Year Benchmark Test

Part 1: Reading

Selection 1: "Linda's Invention"

1. Possible answers: in a city, in a city neighborhood, in front of an apartment building
2. B
3. A
4. B
5. Wording may vary. Possible answer: She thinks it is a good idea.
6. C
7. A
8. B
9. Wording may vary. Possible answers: She cared about what the city looked like. She wanted to do something about the mess.
10. A
11. C
12. B
13. C
14. C
15. B
16. C
17. A

Selection 2: "About Dr. Seuss"

18. B
19. C
20. B
21. Wording may vary. Possible answers: He worked hard to make them better. He wanted them to be good.
22. Wording may vary. Possible answers: He was an older man; he had a beard; he wore glasses.
23. C
24. Possible answers: They sent him a lot of mail; they sent him green eggs and ham.
25. A
26. B
27. C
28. A
29. B
30. A
31. C
32. A
33. C
34. A
35. B

End-of-Year
Benchmark Test, *continued*

Part 2: Responding to Literature
Scoring Guide: How-to Paragraph

4 Exemplary

The paragraph explains how to make "The Garbage Game" or how to write a letter. The task is defined, and ample information is provided. The explanation includes three to five steps and uses words such as *first* to indicate order of steps. A how-to for "The Garbage Game," for example, might include finding a large box, cutting a hole in the top, and writing or painting words on the side (such as "Toss and win"). Errors in grammar, usage, and mechanics are minimal and do not affect meaning.

3 Competent

The paragraph explains how to make "The Garbage Game" or how to write a letter. The writer attempts to define the task, and adequate information is provided. The explanation includes three or four steps and uses words such as *first* to indicate order of steps. It may include a few errors in grammar, usage, and mechanics, but they do not affect meaning.

2 Developing

The paragraph attempts to explain how to make "The Garbage Game" or how to write a letter, but the task may be unclear. A step may be missing from the explanation, or steps may be unclear. More words such as *first* are needed to indicate order of steps. There may be several errors in grammar, usage, and mechanics, which may affect meaning.

1 Emerging

The piece does not explain how to make "The Garbage Game" or write a letter, or it does not accurately reflect the content of the selection. Errors in grammar, usage, and mechanics obscure meaning.

TESTED SKILLS

These charts indicate the skill tested by each item in the Benchmark Tests. You may want to use these lists to help analyze students' responses to specific test questions.

Unit 1: You + Me = Special

Part 1: Reading

1. Predicting
2. Character
3. Setting
4. Character
5. Setting
6. Author's purpose
7. Critical thinking: Making judgments
8. Initial *l, r, s* blends
9. Initial consonant digraphs
10. Final consonant digraphs
11. Predicting
12. Setting
13. Character
14. Character
15. Author's purpose
16. Genre
17. Long vowels: /ē/ *ea, ee*
18. Long vowels with final *e*
19. Critical thinking: Making judgments
20. Critical thinking: Comparing and contrasting across texts

Part 2: Responding to Literature

Prompt: Writing a story about me

Unit 2: Zoom In!

Part 1: Reading

1. Sequence of events
2. Using graphic sources
3. Drawing conclusions
4. Drawing conclusions
5. Predicting
6. Critical thinking: Synthesizing ideas
7. Critical thinking: Making judgments
8. Long vowels: /a/ *ai, ay*
9. Medial consonants
10. Inflected endings: *-es, -ing, -s*
11. Drawing conclusions
12. Critical thinking: Comparing and contrasting
13. Steps in a process
14. Using graphic sources
15. Steps in a process
16. Critical thinking: Making judgments
17. Critical thinking: Synthesizing ideas
18. *r*-controlled vowels: /ėr/*er, ur*
19. Compound words
20. Critical thinking: Comparing and contrasting across texts

Part 2: Responding to Literature

Prompt: Writing a descriptive paragraph

TESTED SKILLS

Unit 3: Side by Side

Part 1: Reading

1. Character
2. Setting
3. Critical thinking: Inferring
4. Context clues
5. Summarizing
6. Comparing and contrasting
7. Drawing conclusions
8. *r*-controlled vowels: /ôr/ *or, oor*
9. Vowel patterns: *ew, oo*
10. Possessives
11. Drawing conclusions
12. Setting
13. Summarizing
14. Comparing and contrasting
15. Context clues
16. Comparing and contrasting
17. Character
18. Vowel diphthongs: *ou, ow*
19. Consonants: /z/ *se*
20. Critical thinking: Comparing and contrasting across texts

Part 2: Responding to Literature

Prompt: Writing a narrative paragraph

Unit 4: Ties Through Time

Part 1: Reading

1. Plot
2. Steps in a process
3. Context clues
4. Cause/effect
5. Classifying
6. Critical thinking: Inferring
7. Cause/effect
8. *r*-controlled vowels: /ir/ *ear, eer*
9. Vowels: /ò/ *a, al, ough*
10. Silent consonants: *wh*
11. Plot
12. Cause/effect
13. Setting
14. Context clues
15. Critical thinking: Inferring
16. Classifying
17. Critical thinking: Making judgments
18. Comparative endings: *-er, -est*
19. Suffixes: *-ly, -ful*
20. Critical thinking: Comparing and contrasting across texts

Part 2: Responding to Literature

Prompt: Writing a journal entry

Unit 5: All Aboard!

Part 1: Reading

1. Plot
2. Character
3. Context clues
4. Critical thinking: Inferring
5. Character
6. Comparing and contrasting
7. Drawing conclusions
8. Plurals: *-s* and *-es*
9. Long vowels: /ā/ *ei*
10. Plurals: *-s* and *-es*
11. Main idea and supporting details
12. Classifying/categorizing
13. Steps in a process
14. Context clues
15. Graphic sources
16. Comparing and contrasting
17. Fact and opinion
18. Short vowels: /u/ *ou*
19. Vowel digraphs: /ü/ *ue*
20. Critical thinking: Comparing and contrasting across texts

Part 2: Responding to Literature

Prompt: Writing an explanatory paragraph

Unit 6: Just Imagine!

Part 1: Reading

1. Plot
2. Plot
3. Context clues
4. Setting
5. Theme
6. Realism and fantasy
7. Critical thinking: Making judgments
8. Character
9. Consonants: /sk/ *sch*
10. *r*-controlled vowels: /âr/*air, are*
11. Plot
12. Cause and effect
13. Context clues
14. Theme
15. Critical thinking: Making judgments
16. Realism and fantasy
17. Consonants: /f/ *gh, ph*
18. Long vowels at ends of syllables
19. Plurals: *-es* (*f* to *v*)
20. Critical thinking: Comparing and contrasting across texts

Part 2: Responding to Literature

Prompt: Writing a friendly letter

End-of-Year
Benchmark Test

Part 1: Reading

1. Setting
2. Character
3. Context clues
4. Sequence of events
5. Drawing conclusions
6. Critical thinking: Inferring
7. Predicting
8. Theme
9. Comparing and contrasting
10. Critical thinking: Making judgments
11. Long vowels: /ā/ *ai, ay*
12. *r*-controlled vowels: /är/ *ar*
13. Silent consonants: *wr*
14. Consonants: /f/ *gh*
15. Compound words
16. Possessives
17. Comparative endings: *-er, -est*
18. Main idea and supporting details
19. Author's purpose
20. Context clues
21. Cause and effect
22. Using graphic sources
23. Fact and opinion
24. Critical thinking: Making judgments
25. Main idea and supporting details
26. Critical thinking: Comparing and contrasting across texts
27. Critical thinking: Comparing and contrasting across texts
28. Silent consonants: *gn*
29. Long vowels: /ē/ *ea, ee*
30. Consonants: /k/ *ch*
31. Vowel diphthongs: *ou, ow*
32. Vowels: /ȯ/ *aw, ough*
33. Plurals: *-s* and *-es*
34. Inflected endings: *-ing*
35. Contractions

Part 2: Responding to Literature
Prompt: Writing a how-to paragraph